# Richard Harwood and Ian Lodge

## Cambridge IGCSE®

# Chemistry

## Workbook

## Fourth edition

CAMBRIDGE
UNIVERSITY PRESS

# CAMBRIDGE
## UNIVERSITY PRESS

University Printing House, Cambridge CB2 8BS, United Kingdom

Cambridge University Press is part of the University of Cambridge.

It furthers the University's mission by disseminating knowledge in the pursuit of education, learning and research at the highest international levels of excellence.

Information on this title: education.cambridge.org

First published 1998
Second edition 2002
Third edition 2010
Fourth edition 2014
3rd printing 2015

Printed by Multivista Global Ltd, India

*A catalogue record for this publication is available from the British Library*

ISBN 978-1-107-61499-4 Paperback

......................................................................................

......................................................................................

® IGCSE is the registered trademark of Cambridge International Examinations.

The questions and example answers in this book were written by the authors.

Cover image: David Taylor / SPL

All artworks © Cambridge University Press

# Contents

# Introduction

This workbook contains exercises designed to help you to develop the skills you need to do well in your IGCSE Chemistry examination.

The IGCSE examination tests three different Assessment Objectives. These are:

**AO1** Knowledge with understanding
**AO2** Handling information and problem solving
**AO3** Experimental skills and investigations

In the examination, about 50% of the marks are for objective AO1, 30% for objective AO2 and 20% for AO3.

Just learning your work and remembering it is, therefore, not enough to make sure that you get the best possible grade in the exam. Half of all the marks are for objectives AO2 and AO3. You need to be able to use what you have learnt and apply it in unfamiliar contexts (AO2) and to demonstrate experimental and data handling skills (AO3).

There are lots of exam-style questions in your coursebook which, together with the material on the accompanying CD-ROM, are aimed at helping you to develop the examination skills necessary to achieve your potential in the exams. Chapter **12** in the coursebook also deals with the experimental skills you will need to apply during your course. This workbook adds detailed exercises to help you further. There are some questions that simply involve remembering things you have been taught (AO1), but most of the exercises require you to use what you have learned to extend your knowledge to novel situations that you have not met before, or to work out, for example, what a set of data means, and indeed to suggest how an experiment might be improved: they are aimed at developing objectives AO2 and AO3. Chemistry is a subject where it is important to understand the connections between the ideas involved. So, while each exercise has a focus on a particular topic, the questions will take you to different connected areas of the subject. There are also exercises, particularly in Chapter 12, aimed at developing your skills in planning practical investigations; an important area of objective AO3.

There are a good many opportunities for you to draw graphs, read scales, interpret data and draw conclusions. These skills are heavily examined in alternative to practical written examinations and so need continuous practice to get them right. Self-assessment check lists are provided to enable you to judge your work according to criteria similar to those used by examiners. You can try marking your own work using these. This will help you to remember the important points to think about. Your teacher should also mark the work, and will discuss with you whether your own assessments are right.

The workbook follows the same chapter breakdown as the coursebook. It is not intended that you should necessarily do the exercises in the order printed, but that you should do them as needed during your course. There are questions from all sections of the syllabus and one aim has been to give a broad range of examples of how the syllabus material is used in exam questions. The workbook is aimed at helping all students that are taking the Chemistry course.

**S** The exercises cover both Core and Supplement material of the syllabus. The Supplement material can be identified by the Supplement symbol in the margin (as shown). This indicates that the exercise is intended for students who are studying the Supplement content of the syllabus as well as the Core.

**A** Some exercises contain additional information that will not be examined, but will help develop your scientific skills and broaden your knowledge. These are identified by the Additional symbol in the margin (as shown).

We trust that the range and differing approaches of the exercises will help you develop a good understanding of the course material and the skills to do really well in the exams.

# The Periodic Table

**Key**

| | |
|---|---|
| a | a = relative atomic mass |
| **X** | X = atomic symbol |
| b | b = proton (atomic) number |

| Group I | II | | | | | | | | | | | | III | IV | V | VI | VII | VIII / 0 |
|---|---|---|---|---|---|---|---|---|---|---|---|---|---|---|---|---|---|---|
| | | | | | | **H**<br>Hydrogen<br>1 | | | | | | | | | | | | **He** 2<br>Helium<br>4 |
| **Li** 3<br>Lithium<br>7 | **Be** 4<br>Beryllium<br>9 | | | | | | | | | | | | **B** 5<br>Boron<br>11 | **C** 6<br>Carbon<br>12 | **N** 7<br>Nitrogen<br>14 | **O** 8<br>Oxygen<br>16 | **F** 9<br>Fluorine<br>19 | **Ne** 10<br>Neon<br>20 |
| **Na** 11<br>Sodium<br>23 | **Mg** 12<br>Magnesium<br>24 | | | | | | | | | | | | **Al** 13<br>Aluminium<br>27 | **Si** 14<br>Silicon<br>28 | **P** 15<br>Phosphorus<br>31 | **S** 16<br>Sulfur<br>32 | **Cl** 17<br>Chlorine<br>35.5 | **Ar** 18<br>Argon<br>40 |
| **K** 19<br>Potassium<br>39 | **Ca** 20<br>Calcium<br>40 | **Sc** 21<br>Scandium<br>45 | **Ti** 22<br>Titanium<br>48 | **V** 23<br>Vanadium<br>51 | **Cr** 24<br>Chromium<br>52 | **Mn** 25<br>Manganese<br>55 | **Fe** 26<br>Iron<br>56 | **Co** 27<br>Cobalt<br>59 | **Ni** 28<br>Nickel<br>59 | **Cu** 29<br>Copper<br>64 | **Zn** 30<br>Zinc<br>65 | | **Ga** 31<br>Gallium<br>70 | **Ge** 32<br>Germanium<br>73 | **As** 33<br>Arsenic<br>75 | **Se** 34<br>Selenium<br>79 | **Br** 35<br>Bromine<br>80 | **Kr** 36<br>Krypton<br>84 |
| **Rb** 37<br>Rubidium<br>85 | **Sr** 38<br>Strontium<br>88 | **Y** 39<br>Yttrium<br>89 | **Zr** 40<br>Zirconium<br>91 | **Nb** 41<br>Niobium<br>93 | **Mo** 42<br>Molybdenum<br>96 | **Tc** 43<br>Technetium<br>– | **Ru** 44<br>Ruthenium<br>101 | **Rh** 45<br>Rhodium<br>103 | **Pd** 46<br>Palladium<br>106 | **Ag** 47<br>Silver<br>108 | **Cd** 48<br>Cadmium<br>112 | | **In** 49<br>Indium<br>115 | **Sn** 50<br>Tin<br>119 | **Sb** 51<br>Antimony<br>122 | **Te** 52<br>Tellurium<br>128 | **I** 53<br>Iodine<br>127 | **Xe** 54<br>Xenon<br>131 |
| **Cs** 55<br>Caesium<br>133 | **Ba** 56<br>Barium<br>137 | **La** 57 *<br>Lanthanum<br>139 | **Hf** 72<br>Hafnium<br>179 | **Ta** 73<br>Tantalum<br>181 | **W** 74<br>Tungsten<br>184 | **Re** 75<br>Rhenium<br>186 | **Os** 76<br>Osmium<br>190 | **Ir** 77<br>Iridium<br>192 | **Pt** 78<br>Platinum<br>195 | **Au** 79<br>Gold<br>197 | **Hg** 80<br>Mercury<br>201 | | **Tl** 81<br>Thallium<br>204 | **Pb** 82<br>Lead<br>207 | **Bi** 83<br>Bismuth<br>209 | **Po** 84<br>Polonium<br>209 | **At** 85<br>Astatine<br>210 | **Rn** 86<br>Radon<br>222 |
| **Fr** 87<br>Francium<br>223 | **Ra** 88<br>Radium<br>226 | **Ac** 89 †<br>Actinium<br>227 | **Rf** 104<br>Rutherfordium<br>261 | **Db** 105<br>Dubnium<br>262 | **Sg** 106<br>Seaborgium<br>263 | **Bh** 107<br>Bohrium<br>264 | **Hs** 108<br>Hassium<br>265 | **Mt** 109<br>Meitnerium<br>268 | **Ds** 110<br>Darmstadtium<br>281 | **Rg** 111<br>Roentgenium<br>273 | **Cn** 112<br>Copernicium<br>– | | **Uut** 113<br>Ununtrium<br>– | **Fl** 114<br>Flerovium<br>– | **Uup** 115<br>Ununpentium<br>– | **Lv** 116<br>Livermorium<br>– | **Uus** 117<br>Ununseptium<br>– | **Uuo** 118<br>Ununoctium<br>– |

\*58–71 Lanthanoid series

| **Ce** 58<br>Cerium<br>140 | **Pr** 59<br>Praseodymium<br>141 | **Nd** 60<br>Neodymium<br>144 | **Pm** 61<br>Promethium<br>145 | **Sm** 62<br>Samarium<br>150 | **Eu** 63<br>Europium<br>152 | **Gd** 64<br>Gadolinium<br>157 | **Tb** 65<br>Terbium<br>159 | **Dy** 66<br>Dysprosium<br>163 | **Ho** 67<br>Holmium<br>165 | **Er** 68<br>Erbium<br>167 | **Tm** 69<br>Thulium<br>169 | **Yb** 70<br>Ytterbium<br>173 | **Lu** 71<br>Lutetium<br>175 |
|---|---|---|---|---|---|---|---|---|---|---|---|---|---|

†90–103 Actinoid series

| **Th** 90<br>Thorium<br>232 | **Pa** 91<br>Protactinium<br>231 | **U** 92<br>Uranium<br>238 | **Np** 93<br>Neptunium<br>237 | **Pu** 94<br>Plutonium<br>244 | **Am** 95<br>Americium<br>243 | **Cm** 96<br>Curium<br>247 | **Bk** 97<br>Berkelium<br>247 | **Cf** 98<br>Californium<br>251 | **Es** 99<br>Einsteinium<br>252 | **Fm** 100<br>Fermium<br>257 | **Md** 101<br>Mendelevium<br>258 | **No** 102<br>Nobelium<br>259 | **Lr** 103<br>Lawrencium<br>262 |
|---|---|---|---|---|---|---|---|---|---|---|---|---|---|

# 1 Planet Earth

## Definitions to learn

- **acid rain**  rainfall with a pH usually less than 5 resulting from dissolved atmospheric pollution
- **greenhouse gas**  a gas which absorbs heat (infrared radiation) and keeps the surface of the planet warm
- **photosynthesis**  the photochemical reaction in the green leaves of plants that turns carbon dioxide and water into glucose and oxygen
- **respiration**  the biochemical reaction in living cells that produces energy from the reaction of glucose and oxygen to produce carbon dioxide and water

## Useful equations

carbon dioxide + water $\rightarrow$ glucose + oxygen     $6CO_2 + 6H_2O \rightarrow C_6H_{12}O_6 + 6O_2$     photosynthesis

glucose + oxygen $\rightarrow$ carbon dioxide + water     $C_6H_{12}O_6 + 6O_2 \rightarrow 6CO_2 + 6H_2O$     respiration

## Exercise 1.1    Global warming and the 'greenhouse effect'

This exercise will help in developing your skills at processing unfamiliar data and making deductions from novel sources.

The diagram shows a simplified carbon cycle.

**a**   Describe the process of photosynthesis in simple terms.

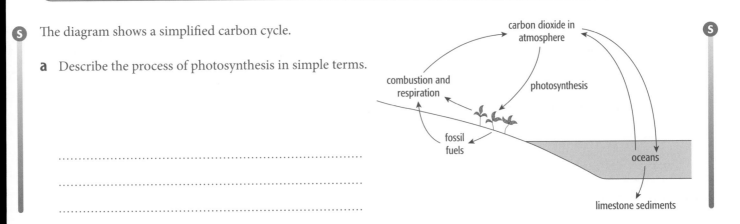

.........................................................................

.........................................................................

.........................................................................

The '**greenhouse effect**' is caused by heat from the Sun being trapped inside the Earth's atmosphere by some of the gases which are present – their molecules absorb infrared radiation. As the amount of these 'greenhouse gases' increases, the mean (average) temperature of the Earth increases. It is estimated that, if there were no 'greenhouse effect,' the Earth's temperature would be cooler by 33 °C on average. Some of the gases which cause this effect are carbon dioxide, methane and oxides of nitrogen ($NO_x$).

Global warming: Since the burning of fossil fuels started to increase in the late nineteenth century, the amount of carbon dioxide in the atmosphere has increased steadily. The changes in the mean temperature of the Earth have not been quite so regular. Below are some data regarding the changes in mean temperature of the Earth and amount of carbon dioxide in the atmosphere. The first table (Table 1) gives the changes over recent years, while the second table gives the longer-term changes (Table 2). The mean temperature is the average over all parts of the Earth's surface over a whole year. The amount of carbon dioxide is given in ppm (parts of carbon dioxide per million parts of air).

| Year | $CO_2$ / ppm | Mean temperature / °C |
|------|--------------|-----------------------|
| 1982 | 340 | 14.08 |
| 1984 | 343 | 14.15 |
| 1986 | 347 | 14.19 |
| 1988 | 351 | 14.41 |
| 1990 | 354 | 14.48 |
| 1992 | 356 | 14.15 |
| 1994 | 358 | 14.31 |
| 1996 | 361 | 14.36 |
| 1998 | 366 | 14.70 |
| 2000 | 369 | 14.39 |
| 2002 | 373 | 14.67 |
| 2004 | 377 | 14.58 |
| 2006 | 381 | 14.63 |
| 2008 | 385 | 14.51 |
| 2010 | 390 | 14.69 |
| 2012 | 394 | 14.59 |

Table 1

| Year | $CO_2$ / ppm | Mean temperature / °C |
|------|--------------|-----------------------|
| 1880 | 291 | 13.92 |
| 1890 | 294 | 13.81 |
| 1900 | 297 | 13.95 |
| 1910 | 300 | 13.80 |
| 1920 | 303 | 13.82 |
| 1930 | 306 | 13.96 |
| 1940 | 309 | 14.14 |
| 1950 | 312 | 13.83 |
| 1960 | 317 | 13.99 |
| 1970 | 324 | 14.04 |
| 1980 | 338 | 14.28 |

Table 2

**b** Plot these results on the grid using the left-hand $y$-axis for amount of carbon dioxide and the right-hand $y$-axis for mean temperature. Draw two separate graphs to enable you to compare the trends. (Use graph paper if you need a larger grid.)

**c** What do you notice about the trend in amount of carbon dioxide?

.................................................................................................................................................................

.................................................................................................................................................................

**d** What do you notice about the trend in mean temperature?

.................................................................................................................................................................

.................................................................................................................................................................

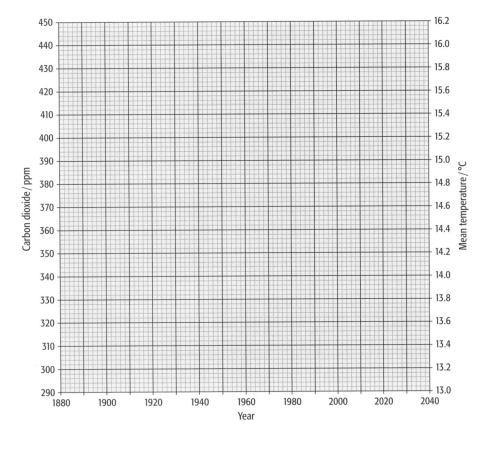

**e** Does the graph clearly show that an increase in carbon dioxide is causing an increase in temperature?

.................................................................................................................................

.................................................................................................................................

**f** Estimate the amount of carbon dioxide in the atmosphere and the likely mean temperature of the Earth in the years 2020 and 2040.

.................................................................................................................................

.................................................................................................................................

**g** Between the eleventh century and the end of the eighteenth century the amount of carbon dioxide in the atmosphere varied between 275 and 280 ppm. Why did it start to rise from the nineteenth century onwards.

.................................................................................................................................

**h** Other 'greenhouse gases' are present in much smaller amounts. However, they are much more effective at keeping in heat than carbon dioxide. Methane (1.7 ppm) has 21 times the effect of carbon dioxide. Nitrogen oxides (0.3 ppm) have 310 times the effect of carbon dioxide.

Name a source that releases each of these gases into the atmosphere.

Methane: .................................................................................................................

Nitrogen oxides: .....................................................................................................

Use the checklist below to give yourself a mark for your graph.
For each point, award yourself:
2 marks if you did it really well
1 mark if you made a good attempt at it, and partly succeeded
0 marks if you did not try to do it, or did not succeed.

**Self-assessment checklist for graphs:**

| Check point | Marks awarded | |
| --- | --- | --- |
| | You | Your teacher |
| You have plotted each point precisely and correctly for both sets of data – using the different scales on the two vertical axes. | | |
| You have used a small, neat cross or dot for the points of one graph. | | |
| You have used a small, but different, symbol for the points of the other graph. | | |
| You have drawn the connecting lines through one set of points accurately – using a ruler for the lines. | | |
| You have drawn the connecting lines through the other set of points accurately – using a different colour or broken line. | | |
| You have ignored any anomalous results when drawing the lines. | | |
| Total (out of 12) | | |

10–12  Excellent.
7–9    Good.
4–6    A good start, but you need to improve quite a bit.
2–3    Poor. Try this same graph again, using a new sheet of graph paper.
1      Very poor. Read through all the criteria again, and then try the same
       graph again.

# Exercise 1.2   Atmospheric pollution, industry and transport

> This exercise discusses different aspects of atmospheric pollution and relates it to key aspects of human activity. It will help you in developing your skills in evaluating data and drawing conclusions from them.

The following pie charts show estimates of the sources of three major atmospheric pollutants in an industrialised country.

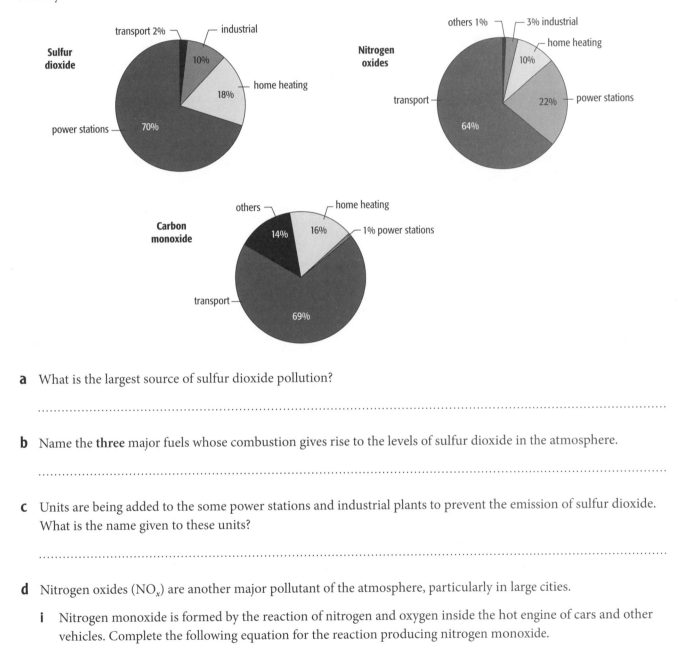

**a** What is the largest source of sulfur dioxide pollution?

..................................................................................................................................................................

**b** Name the **three** major fuels whose combustion gives rise to the levels of sulfur dioxide in the atmosphere.

..................................................................................................................................................................

**c** Units are being added to the some power stations and industrial plants to prevent the emission of sulfur dioxide. What is the name given to these units?

..................................................................................................................................................................

**d** Nitrogen oxides ($NO_x$) are another major pollutant of the atmosphere, particularly in large cities.

   **i** Nitrogen monoxide is formed by the reaction of nitrogen and oxygen inside the hot engine of cars and other vehicles. Complete the following equation for the reaction producing nitrogen monoxide.

$$N_2 + O_2 \rightarrow \ldots\ldots NO$$

**ii** When leaving the car, nitrogen monoxide in the exhaust fumes reacts further with oxygen in the air to produce the brown gas which can be seen in the atmosphere over large cities. This gas is nitrogen dioxide. Balance the equation for the production of this gas.

$$\text{nitrogen monoxide} + \text{oxygen} \rightarrow \text{nitrogen dioxide}$$

$$\ldots\ldots NO \quad + \quad O_2 \quad \rightarrow \quad \ldots\ldots NO_2$$

**iii** The operating temperature of a diesel engine is significantly higher than that of a petrol (gasoline) engine. Would you expect the level of $NO_x$ emissions from a diesel-powered vehicle to be greater or lower than from a petrol-powered vehicle? Give the reason for your answer.

.................................................................................................................................................

.................................................................................................................................................

**iv** What attachment is fitted to modern cars to reduce the level of pollution by oxides of nitrogen?

.................................................................................................................................................

**e** Nitrogen oxides, unburnt hydrocarbons and carbon monoxide combine together under the influence of ultraviolet light to produce photochemical smog.

**i** Why do you think this form of pollution is most common in large cities?

.................................................................................................................................................

.................................................................................................................................................

**ii** What other form of pollution from car exhaust fumes has now almost totally disappeared from modern cities following changes in fuel and pollution monitoring?

.................................................................................................................................................

**f** In order to control traffic flow, London introduced a 'congestion charge' for vehicles entering the centre of the city in 2003. The table shows figures for the percentage fall in the levels of certain pollutants following the introduction of the congestion charge.

| | Pollutant gas within Congestion Charge Zone | |
|---|---|---|
| | $NO_x$ | $CO_2$ |
| Overall traffic emissions change 2003 versus 2002 / % | −13.4 | −16.4 |
| Overall traffic emissions change 2004 versus 2003 / % | −5.2 | −0.9 |
| Change due to improved vehicle technology, 2003 to 2006 / % | −17.3 | −3.4 |

**i** What was the measured percentage drop in the level of nitrogen oxides within the Congestion Charge Zone over the first two years following the introduction of the charge?

.................................................................................................................................................

.................................................................................................................................................

**ii**   At face value there seems to be a drop in the levels of pollutants following the introduction of the congestion charge. But should we expect the fall in pollution levels to continue?

.................................................................................................................................................................

**iii**   An independent study published in 2011 suggested that other factors should be taken into account, particularly when trying to study a relatively small area within a large city. One factor is hinted at in the third row of figures. What is that factor; and what other influences need to be taken into account in considering this situation?

.................................................................................................................................................................

.................................................................................................................................................................

.................................................................................................................................................................

.................................................................................................................................................................

**g**   The use of fossil fuels in industry and transport also produces carbon dioxide. What is the reasoning behind the slogan painted on these freight containers seen waiting to be loaded on to a freight train outside a major UK station? Outline the argument behind the slogan.

.................................................................................................................................................................

.................................................................................................................................................................

.................................................................................................................................................................

.................................................................................................................................................................

.................................................................................................................................................................

.................................................................................................................................................................

# Exercise 1.3    Clean water is crucial

> This exercise covers aspects of how we produce clean water for domestic and industrial use, focusing on stages that depend on key physical and chemical techniques.

The provision of clean drinking water and sanitation to more of the world's population is one of the key millennium goals of the United Nations. The lack of this basic provision impacts not only on the levels of disease in an area, in particular the mortality rate of children, but also on the level of education and the role of women within a community.

The diagram shows the different stages involved in a modern water plant producing water for domestic and industrial use.

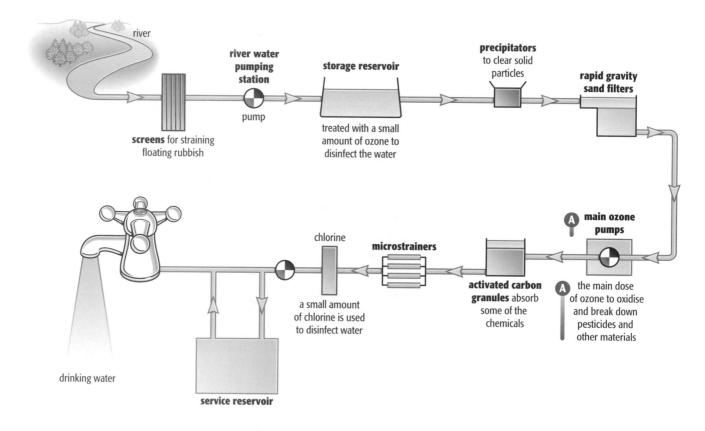

a   What devices are used in the early stages of processing to remove insoluble debris and material? Include comments on the size of the material removed by these methods.

................................................................................................................................................

................................................................................................................................................

................................................................................................................................................

b   What is the common purpose of treating the water with chlorine and/or ozone?

................................................................................................................................................

**c** What other purpose does treatment with ozone achieve?

.................................................................................................................................................

**d** What type of chemical agent is ozone ($O_3$) behaving as in the reactions involved in part c?

.................................................................................................................................................

**e** Countries that have insufficient rainfall, or where water supply is in great demand, may need to use other methods of producing clean water. Here, processes for **desalination** are used.

   **i** What does the term **desalination** mean?

   .................................................................................................................................................

   **ii** Name **two** methods that such countries use for desalination.

   .................................................................................................................................................

   **iii** Give **one** disadvantage of these methods of desalination.

   .................................................................................................................................................

**f** Tap water produced by this type of treatment is clean, but it is not pure. It will contain metal and non-metal ions dissolved from the rocks that the rivers and streams have flowed over.

   **i** Chloride ions are present in tap water. Describe a chemical test that would show the presence of chloride ions ($Cl^-$) in the water. Describe the test and what would be observed.

   .................................................................................................................................................

   .................................................................................................................................................

   .................................................................................................................................................

   **ii** One of the chlorides often present in tap water is sodium chloride. Give the word and balanced symbol equation for the reaction taking place in the test you have described above.

      sodium chloride  +  ..............  →  ..............  +  ..............

                     ..............        ..............       ..............

      NaCl              +  ..............  →  ..............  +  ..............

   **iii** Give the ionic equation for the reaction taking place (include state symbols).

   .................................................................................................................................................

# Exercise 1.4   Gases in the air

This exercise discusses how the composition of the Earth's atmosphere has been influenced by volcanic emissions over the duration of the life of the planet. It looks at how the composition of the atmosphere has changed and how we purify the different gases from the air.

There have been several spectacular volcanic eruptions in recent years. In 2010, clouds of ash from the relatively small eruption of the Eyjafjallajokoll volcano in Iceland caused disruption in most of European airspace throughout the month of April.

The diagram shows the spread of the volcanic ash cloud over Europe during April 2010.

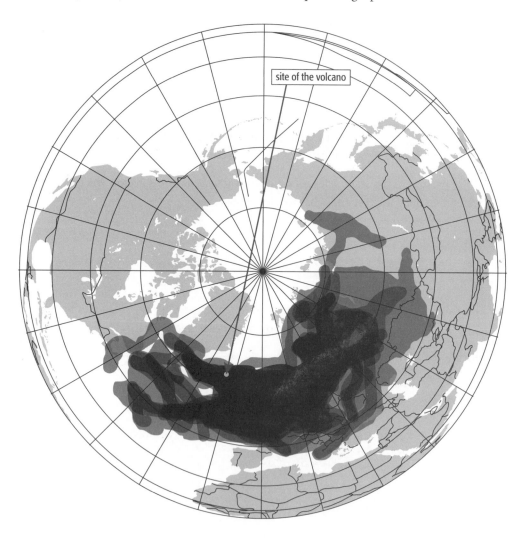

Active volcanoes produce many unseen products which are thrown out into the atmosphere. The table below shows the gases released by an active Icelandic volcano.

| Name of gas | Percentage of total gas released / % |
|---|---|
| sulfur dioxide | 11.70 |
| nitrogen | 3.20 |
| water vapour | 35.60 |
| hydrogen | 0.39 |
| carbon dioxide | 47.40 |
| carbon monoxide | 1.71 |

a Which gas is present in the largest quantity in the gases released by the volcano?

.................................................................................................................................................

b Explain why water is in the gas phase when it comes out of the volcano.

.................................................................................................................................................

c Comment on what happens to the hydrogen released from the volcano. Why is it not kept within the Earth's atmosphere?

.................................................................................................................................................

It is now recognised that the early atmosphere of the Earth was generated by release of gases from volcanoes. The composition of air has changed significantly over millions of years. The following table shows how the composition of the atmosphere has changed since the formation of the planet 4500 million years ago.

| | Time in the past / million years | Approximate proportion of carbon dioxide / % | Approximate proportion of oxygen / % | Approximate proportion of gas X / % |
|---|---|---|---|---|
| present | 0 | 0.04 | 20 | 79 |
| | 500 | 1 | 20 | 78 |
| | 1000 | 2 | 19 | 77 |
| | 1500 | 5 | 18 | 75 |
| | 2000 | 7 | 10 | 70 |
| | 2500 | 10 | 5 | 60 |
| | 3000 | 15 | 1 | 55 |
| | 3500 | 21 | 0.5 | 40 |
| | 4000 | 40 | 0 | 30 |
| formation | 4500 | 90 | 0 | 10 |

**d** Using the grid below, draw graphs of how the proportions of the three gases listed in the table have changed over time from the origin of the Earth.

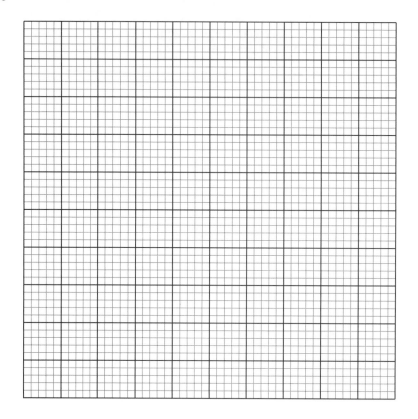

**e** Identify gas **X**, giving your reasoning.

.................................................................................................................................................................................................

.................................................................................................................................................................................................

**Ⓐ f** Water vapour is released by volcanoes as a gas. What eventually happened to the water vapour in the atmosphere?

.................................................................................................................................................................................................

.................................................................................................................................................................................................

**g** Mark arrows on the timeline of your graph to indicate the points at which the following occurred:

**i** the oceans were formed

**ii** the first forms of bacteria (including photosynthesising algae) appeared

**iii** vegetation on land appeared.

**Ⓢ h** Explain why the appearance of photosynthetic algae, followed by land vegetation and plants, caused a change in the level of carbon dioxide present in the air.

.................................................................................................................................................................................................

.................................................................................................................................................................................................

.................................................................................................................................................................................................

**S** **i** The gases in the atmosphere can be separated and purified by fractional distillation of liquid air. Dust-free air is cooled to around −80 °C to remove water and carbon dioxide. The air is then cooled to −200 °C at high pressure to liquefy it. The table shows the boiling points of the gases involved.

| Gas | Boiling point / °C |
| --- | --- |
| argon | −186 |
| helium | −269 |
| krypton | −157 |
| neon | −246 |
| nitrogen | −196 |
| oxygen | −183 |
| xenon | −108 |

**i** Which gases will not become liquid at −200 °C?

.................................................................................................................................................

**ii** Outline how the liquid air is separated by fractional distillation, stating clearly which gas will be the first to distil over?

.................................................................................................................................................

.................................................................................................................................................

.................................................................................................................................................

.................................................................................................................................................

**iii** Which **two** gases are difficult to separate by this method? Why is this?

.................................................................................................................................................

.................................................................................................................................................

**iv** Give **one** major use each for liquid nitrogen and liquid oxygen.

.................................................................................................................................................

.................................................................................................................................................

# Exercise 1.5   Hydrogen as a fuel

> This exercise introduces hydrogen as an alternative energy source and will help develop your skills at handling information regarding unfamiliar applications.

One of the first buses to use hydrogen as a fuel was operated in Erlangen, Germany, in 1996. The hydrogen was stored in thick pressurised tanks on the roof of the bus.

**a** Describe **two** advantages of using hydrogen as a fuel rather than gasoline (petrol).

.............................................................................................................................................................

.............................................................................................................................................................

**b** Suggest **one** disadvantage of using hydrogen as a fuel.

.............................................................................................................................................................

It is possible to generate electrical energy from hydrogen using a fuel cell. The structure of a typical fuel cell is shown in the diagram.

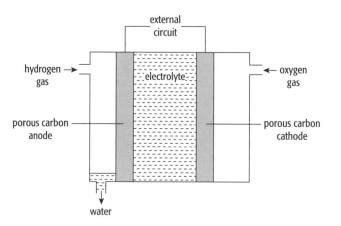

**c** The reaction taking place in such a fuel cell is the combustion of hydrogen. Write the overall equation for that reaction.

.............................................................................................................................................................

**d** The equation for the reaction at the anode is

$$H_2(g) + 2OH^-(aq) \rightarrow 2H_2O(l) + 2e^-$$

What type of reaction is this? Explain your answer.

.............................................................................................................................................................

**e** At the cathode oxygen molecules react with water molecules to form hydroxide ions. Write an ionic equation for this reaction.

.............................................................................................................................................................

# 2 The nature of matter

## Definitions to learn

- **physical state**  the three states of matter are solid, liquid and gas
- **condensation**  the change of state from gas to liquid
- **melting**  the change of state from solid to liquid
- **freezing**  the change of state from liquid to solid at the melting point
- **boiling**  the change of state from liquid to gas at the boiling point of the liquid
- **evaporation**  the change of state from liquid to gas below the boiling point
- **sublimation**  the change of state directly from solid to gas (or the reverse)
- **crystallisation**  the formation of crystals when a saturated solution is left to cool
- **filtration**  the separation of a solid from a liquid using filter paper
- **distillation**  the separation of a liquid from a mixture using differences in boiling point
- **fractional distillation**  the separation of a mixture of liquids using differences in boiling point
- **diffusion**  the random movement of particles in a fluid (liquid or gas) leading to the complete mixing of the particles
- **chromatography**  the separation of a mixture of soluble (coloured) substances using paper and a solvent
- **atom**  the smallest part of an element that can take part in a chemical change
- **proton number (atomic number)**  the number of protons in the nucleus of an atom of an element
- **nucleon number (mass number)**  the number of protons and neutrons in the nucleus of an atom
- **electron arrangement**  the organisation of electrons in their different energy levels (shells)
- **isotopes**  atoms of the same element which have the same proton number but a different nucleon number

## Exercise 2.1   Changing physical state

This exercise will develop your understanding of the kinetic model and the energy changes involved in changes of physical state.

The graph shows the heating curve for a pure substance. The temperature rises with time as the substance is heated.

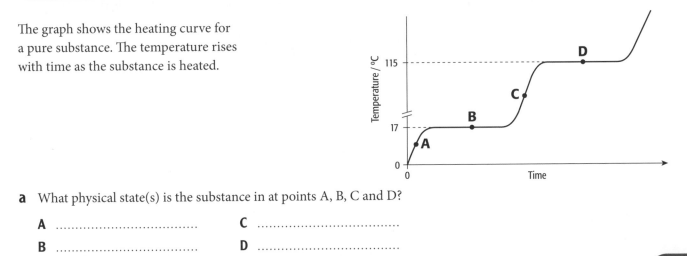

**a**  What physical state(s) is the substance in at points A, B, C and D?

A  .......................................       C  .......................................

B  .......................................       D  .......................................

**b** What is the melting point of the substance? ......................................

**c** What is its boiling point? .....................................

**d** What happens to the temperature while the substance is changing state?

...............................................................................................................................................................

**e** The substance is not water. How do we know this from the graph?

...............................................................................................................................................................

**f** Complete the passage using the words given below.

| different | diffusion | gas | spread | particles |
|-----------|-----------|-----|--------|-----------|
| diffuse | random | lattice | vibrate | temperature |

The kinetic model states that the ..................................... in a liquid and a .....................................

are in constant motion. In a gas, the particles are far apart from each other and their motion is

said to be ..................................... The particles in a solid are held in fixed positions in a regular

..................................... . In a solid, the particles can only ..................................... about their fixed positions.

Liquids and gases are fluid states. When particles move in a fluid, they can collide with each other. When

they collide, they bounce off each other in ..................................... directions. If two gases or liquids are

mixed, the different types of particle ..................................... out and get mixed up. This process is called

..................................... .

**S** At the same ..................................... particles that have a lower mass move faster than those with higher

mass. This means that the lighter particles will spread and mix more quickly; the lighter particles are said to

..................................... faster than the heavier particles.

**g** Use the data given for the substances listed below to answer the questions that follow on their physical state at a
room temperature of 25 °C and atmospheric pressure.

| Substance | Melting point/°C | Boiling point/°C |
|-----------|------------------|------------------|
| sodium | 98 | 883 |
| radon | −71 | −62 |
| ethanol | −117 | 78 |
| cobalt | 1492 | 2900 |
| nitrogen | −210 | −196 |
| propane | −188 | −42 |
| ethanoic acid | 16 | 118 |

**i** Which substance is a liquid over the smallest range of temperature? .....................................

**ii** Which **two** substances are gaseous at −50 °C?

..................................... and .....................................

**iii** Which substance has the lowest freezing point? .....................................

**iv** Which substance is liquid at 2500 °C? .....................................

**v** A sample of ethanoic acid was found to boil at 121 °C at atmospheric pressure. Use the information in the table to comment on this result.

..............................................................................................................................................................

..............................................................................................................................................................

# Exercise 2.2   Plotting a cooling curve

This exercise presents data obtained practically for plotting a cooling curve. It will help develop your skills in handling the data and interpreting what changes the different regions of the curve represent. Examples of sublimation are also discussed.

A student, carried out the following data-logging experiment as part of a project on changes of state. An organic crystalline solid was melted by placing it in a tube in a boiling water bath. A temperature sensor was placed in the liquid.

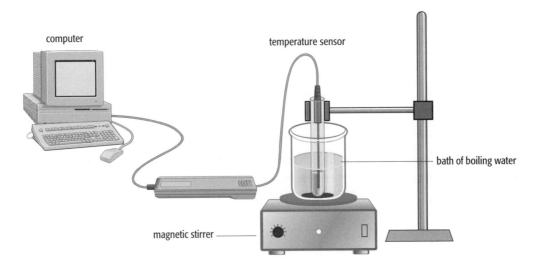

The temperature change was followed as the liquid was allowed to cool down. The data shown in the table below are taken from the computer record of the temperature change as the liquid cooled down to room temperature.

| Time / min | 0 | 0.5 | 1.0 | 1.5 | 2.0 | 2.2 | 2.4 | 2.6 | 2.8 | 3.0 | 3.5 | 4.0 | 4.5 | 5.0 |
|---|---|---|---|---|---|---|---|---|---|---|---|---|---|---|
| Temperature / °C | 96.1 | 89.2 | 85.2 | 82.0 | 80.9 | 80.7 | 80.6 | 80.6 | 80.5 | 80.3 | 78.4 | 74.2 | 64.6 | 47.0 |

**a** On the grid below, plot a graph of the temperature change taking place in this experiment.

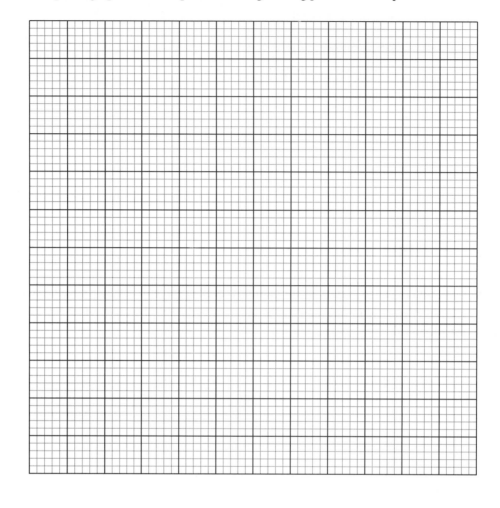

**b** What change is taking place over the second minute of the experiment?

.................................................................................................................................................................................

**c** Why does the temperature remain almost constant over this period of time? Give your explanation in terms of what is happening to the organisation of the molecules of the substance.

.................................................................................................................................................................................

.................................................................................................................................................................................

.................................................................................................................................................................................

.................................................................................................................................................................................

**d** What change would need to be made to carry out the experiment using a compound with a melting point greater than 100 °C?

.................................................................................................................................................................................

**e** A similar experiment was carried out to demonstrate the cooling curve for paraffin wax.

**i** In the space below, sketch the shape of the graph you would expect to produce.

**ii** Explain why the curve is the shape you have drawn.

.................................................................................................................................................

.................................................................................................................................................

**f** Sublimation occurs when a substance passes between the solid and gaseous states without going through the liquid phase. Both carbon dioxide and water can sublime under certain conditions of temperature and pressure.

'Dry ice' is the solid form of carbon dioxide used in commercial refrigeration. At atmospheric pressure it has a 'sublimation point' of −78.5°C.

**i** What difference can you see between solid carbon dioxide and water ice at atmospheric pressure?

......................................................................................................................

......................................................................................................................

**ii** If you gently shake a carbon dioxide fire extinguisher, you will feel the presence of liquid within the extinguisher. What conditions within the extinguisher mean that the $CO_2$ is liquid in this case?

......................................................................................................................

......................................................................................................................

**iii** Complete the following paragraph about a particular type of frost using the words listed below.

| | | | |
|---|---|---|---|
| surrounding | liquid | colder | humid |
| white | crystals | ice | |

Hoar frost is a powdery .............................. frost caused when solid .............................. forms from

.............................. air. The solid surface on which it is formed must be .............................. than the

.............................. air. Water vapour is deposited on a surface as fine ice .............................. without going

through the .............................. phase.

# Exercise 2.3   Diffusion, solubility and separation

> The processes of diffusion and dissolving in a solvent are linked. This exercise explores the basis of these processes in terms of the kinetic (particle) theory. The separation of a solvent mixture by fractional distillation is discussed.

A student placed some crystals of potassium manganate(VII) at the bottom of a beaker of distilled water. She then left the contents of the beaker to stand for one hour.

**a**  The diagram below shows what she saw during the experiment.

After one hour, all the solid crystals had disappeared and the solution was purple throughout.

distilled water

purple crystals

at start          after 15 minutes          after one hour

**i**   Use the ideas of the kinetic theory to explain her observations.

.......................................................................................................................................................

.......................................................................................................................................................

.......................................................................................................................................................

.......................................................................................................................................................

.......................................................................................................................................................

**ii**  If warm water at 50 °C had been used, would the observations have taken place in a longer or shorter time? Explain your answer.

.......................................................................................................................................................

.......................................................................................................................................................

.......................................................................................................................................................

**b**  The process of dissolving can be used to separate and purify chemical compounds. Organic solvents such as propanone can be used to extract pigments from plants. Some grass is crushed and mixed with the propanone. The colour pigments are extracted to give a dark green solution.

**i**   Given a pure sample of chlorophyll, describe how could you show that the green solution from the grass contained chlorophyll and other coloured pigments?

.......................................................................................................................................................

.......................................................................................................................................................

.......................................................................................................................................................

.......................................................................................................................................................

**ii** Draw a labelled diagram that describes the method of separating coloured pigments that you have discussed in part **i**.

Use the checklist below to give yourself a mark for your drawing.

For each point, award yourself:

2 marks if you did it really well

1 mark if you made a good attempt at it, and partly succeeded

0 marks if you did not try to do it, or did not succeed.

**Self-assessment checklist for drawings**

| Check point | Marks awarded | |
| --- | --- | --- |
| | **You** | **Your teacher** |
| You have made a large drawing, using the space provided. | | |
| There are no obvious errors – liquids missing, flasks open when they should be closed, etc. | | |
| You have drawn single lines with a sharp pencil, not many tries at the same line (and erased mistakes). | | |
| You have used a ruler for the lines that are straight. | | |
| Your diagram is in the right proportions. | | |
| You have drawn label lines with a ruler, touching the item being labelled. | | |
| You have written the labels horizontally and neatly, well away from the diagram itself. | | |
| **Total (out of 14)** | | |

12–14   Excellent.

10–11   Good.

7–9      A good start, but you need to improve quite a bit.

5–6      Poor. Try this same drawing again, using a new sheet of paper.

1–4      Very poor. Read through all the criteria again, and then try the same drawing.

**iii** Explain the role of chlorophyll in the leaves of green plants.

...................................................................................................................................................................

...................................................................................................................................................................

...................................................................................................................................................................

...................................................................................................................................................................

**c** Propanone is a very useful solvent that mixes well with water even though it is an organic compound. A propanone:water (65%:35%) mixture used for cleaning laboratory apparatus can be separated using fractional distillation.

A total volume of 80 cm³ of the mixture was distilled.

Sketch below a graph of the temperature readings against the volume of distillate collected for the distillation carried out. The thermometer is placed at the connection between the fractionating column and the condenser. The boiling point of propanone is 56 °C.

# Exercise 2.4    Chromatography at the races

> This exercise will help you understand aspects of chromatography by considering an unfamiliar application of the technique.

Chromatography is used by the 'Horse Racing Forensic Laboratory' to test for the presence of illegal drugs in racehorses.

A concentrated sample of urine is spotted on to chromatography paper on the start line. Alongside this, known drugs are spotted. The chromatogram is run using methanol as the solvent. When finished, the paper is read by placing it under ultraviolet light. A chromatogram of urine from four racehorses is shown below.

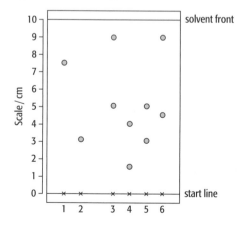

| Spot | Description |
|------|-------------|
| 1 | caffeine |
| 2 | paracetamol |
| 3 | urine sample horse A |
| 4 | urine sample horse B |
| 5 | urine sample horse C |
| 6 | urine sample horse D |

**a** State **two** factors which determine the distance a substance travels up the paper.

......................................................................................................................................................................

......................................................................................................................................................................

**b** The results show that the sample from one horse contains an illegal substance. State which horse and the drug that is present.

......................................................................................................................................................................

**c** Give a reason for the use of this drug.

......................................................................................................................................................................

**d** The results for known drugs are given as '$R_f$ values'.

$$R_f = \frac{\text{distance travelled by the substance}}{\text{distance travelled by the solvent}}$$

Calculate the $R_f$ value for caffeine.

## Exercise 2.5   Atomic structure

> This exercise helps familiarise you with aspects of atomic structure including the organisation of electrons into energy levels (or shells), and the uses of radioactivity.

**a** Choose from the words below to fill in the gaps in the passage. Words may be used once, more than once or not at all.

| proton | electrons | nucleon | isotopes | protons |
|--------|-----------|---------|----------|---------|
| neutrons | nucleus | energy levels | | |

Atoms are made up of three different particles: ................................ which are positively charged;

................................ which have no charge; and ................................ which are negatively charged.

The negatively charged particles are arranged in different ................................ (shells) around the

................................ of the atom. The particles with a negligible mass are the ................................ . All atoms

of the same element contain the same number of ................................ and ................................ . Atoms of the

same element with different numbers of ................................ are known as ................................ .

**b** This part of the exercise is concerned with electron arrangements and the structure of the Periodic Table. Complete these sentences by filling in the blanks with words or numbers.

The electrons in an atom are arranged in a series of .............................. around the

nucleus. These shells are also called ............................. levels. In an atom, the shell

.............................. to the nucleus fills first, then the next shell, and so on. There is

room for:

- up to ............... electrons in the first shell
- up to ............... electrons in the second shell
- up to ............... electrons in the third shell.

(There are 18 electrons in total when the three shells are completely full.)

The elements in the Periodic Table are organised in the same way as the electrons fill the

shells. Shells fill from ............................. to ............................. across

the .............................. of the Periodic Table.

- The first shell fills up first from ............................. to helium.
- The second shell fills next from lithium to ............................. .
- Eight ............................. go into the third shell from sodium to argon.
- Then the fourth shell starts to fill from potassium.

**c** In 1986, an explosion at Chernobyl in the Ukraine released a radioactive cloud containing various radioactive isotopes. Three such isotopes are mentioned below. Use your Periodic Table to answer the following questions about them.

| Element | Nucleon (mass) number |
|---|---|
| strontium | 90 |
| iodine | 131 |
| caesium | 137 |

**i** How many electrons are there in one atom of strontium-90? ..............................

**ii** How many protons are there in one atom cf iodine-131? .............................

**iii** How many neutrons are there in an atom of caesium-137? ............................................

The prevailing winds carried fallout from Chernobyl towards Scandinavia. In Sweden, caesium-137 built up in lichen, which is the food eaten by reindeer. This gave rise to radioactive meat.

**iv** If radioactive caesium was reacted with chlorine, would you expect the caesium chloride produced to be radioactive? Explain your answer.

..........................................................................................................................................................................................................

**v** State a beneficial use in industry of a radioactive isotope.

...............................................................................................................................................................

**vi** State a medical use of a radioactive isotope.

...............................................................................................................................................................

# Exercise 2.6　Influential organisation

> This exercise explores aspects of the discovery of the structure of the atom and how that structure influences the major properties of the atoms of an element.

The way in which the subatomic particles are organised within an atom gives rise to the characteristic properties of that atom. Whether an atom is radioactive, the type of bond it makes, its chemical reactivity and its position in the Periodic Table are all dependent on this organisation.

**a** The modern view of the structure of the atom stems from experiments carried out in Rutherford's laboratory in Manchester, UK. These experiments used α-particles (helium nuclei) fired at a sheet of gold foil from a radioactive source. Detectors analysed the direction of the particles as they passed through the foil. The design of the experiment is summarised in the following diagram.

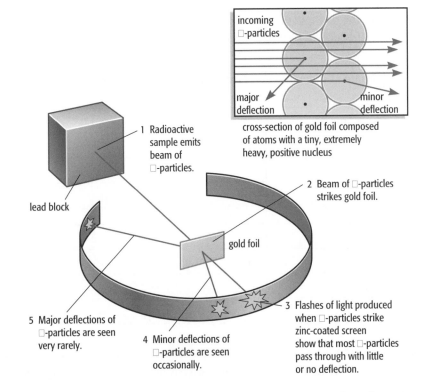

incoming □-particles

major deflection

minor deflection

cross-section of gold foil composed of atoms with a tiny, extremely heavy, positive nucleus

1 Radioactive sample emits beam of □-particles.

lead block

2 Beam of □-particles strikes gold foil.

gold foil

5 Major deflections of □-particles are seen very rarely.

4 Minor deflections of □-particles are seen occasionally.

3 Flashes of light produced when □-particles strike zinc-coated screen show that most □-particles pass through with little or no deflection.

**i** α-particles are helium nuclei. What is the composition of an α-particle and its charge?

Protons: ...............................................

Neutrons: ...............................................

Charge: ...............................................

**ii** Gold foil is a solid metal. How are the atoms of gold arranged in the foil?

.................................................................................................................................................

.................................................................................................................................................

**iii** What did the fact that the majority of the α-particles passed through the foil suggest about the structure of the atoms?

.................................................................................................................................................

.................................................................................................................................................

**iv** Remarkably, some of the α-particles were repelled back in the direction from which they came. What part of the structure of the atom did this suggest the particles had hit, and why were these particles repelled backwards?

.................................................................................................................................................

.................................................................................................................................................

.................................................................................................................................................

**b** The isotopes of certain elements, such as carbon-14, can be of use in biochemical and medical research. Because they are radioactive, they can be used by scientists to track the synthesis and use of compounds important in the chemistry of cells and tissues.

**i** Complete the table about the isotopes of some common elements, making deductions from the information given. For each element, the second isotope is a radioisotope used in research.

| Isotope | Name of element | Proton number | Nucleon number | Number of p | n | e |
|---|---|---|---|---|---|---|
| $^{12}_{6}C$ | carbon | 6 | 12 | 6 | 6 | 6 |
| $^{14}_{6}C$ | | | | | | |
| $^{1}_{1}H$ | | | 1 | | | |
| $^{3}_{1}H$ | hydrogen (tritium) | | | | | |
| $^{31}_{15}P$ | | 15 | 31 | | | |
| $^{32}_{15}P$ | | | | | | |
| $^{127}_{53}I$ | iodine | | | 53 | | 53 |
| $^{131}_{53}I$ | | | | 53 | | |

**ii** Researchers are able to use these radioisotopes to study the chemistry of cells because these atoms have the same chemical properties as the non-radioactive atoms. Why are the chemical properties of all isotopes of the same element identical?

.................................................................................................................................................

.................................................................................................................................................

.................................................................................................................................................

**c** The table below gives details of the atomic structure of five atoms, **A, B, C, D** and **E**. (Note that these letters are **not** their chemical symbols.)

Complete the table to show the electron arrangement of each of the atoms.

| Atom | Proton number | Electron arrangement | | | |
|------|---------------|-----------|-----------|-----------|-----------|
| | | 1st shell | 2nd shell | 3rd shell | 4th shell |
| A | 2 | | | | |
| B | 5 | | | | |
| C | 13 | | | | |
| D | 15 | | | | |
| E | 19 | | | | |

**i** How many of these atoms are of elements in the second period of the Periodic Table?

....................................................................................................................................................................

**ii** Which **two** atoms belong to elements in the same group?

....................................................................................................................................................................

**iii** How many electrons does atom **C** have which would be involved in chemical bonding?

....................................................................................................................................................................

**iv** Draw a diagram to show the arrangement of the electrons in atom **D**.

# 3 Elements and compounds

## Definitions to learn

- **element** a substance containing only one type of atom
- **compound** a substance made of two, or more, elements chemically combined together
- **Periodic Table** the table in which the elements are organised in order of increasing proton number and electron arrangement
- **Group** a vertical column of elements in the Periodic Table; elements in the same group have similar properties
- **Period** a horizontal row of elements in the Periodic Table
- **valency** the number of chemical bonds an atom can make

## Exercise 3.1  Periodic patterns in the properties of the elements

> This exercise will help your understanding of the periodic, or repeating, patterns shown by the elements. It will also support your understanding of the structure of the Periodic Table in groups of elements and help you begin to predict properties within these groups.

One physical property that shows a periodic change linked to the Periodic Table is the melting point of an element. Below is a chart of the melting points of the elements in Periods 2 and 3 plotted against the proton number of the element.

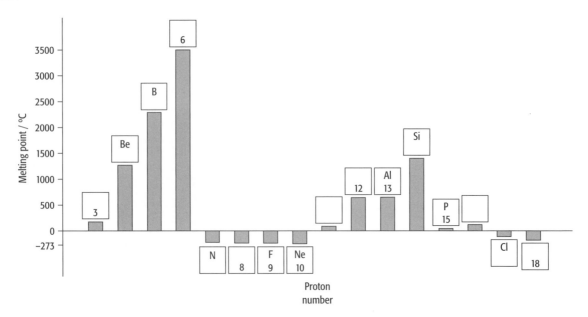

**a** Fill in the symbols and proton numbers missing from the boxes on the chart above (7 symbols and 7 proton numbers).

**b** Which **two** elements are at the peaks of the chart?

..................................... and .....................................

**c** To which group do these two elements belong? .....................................

**d** The halogens are one group of elements in the Periodic Table. Complete the following statements about the halogens by crossing out the incorrect bold words.

- The halogens are **metals / non-metals** and their vapours are **coloured / colourless**.
- The halogens are **toxic / non-toxic** to humans.
- Halogen molecules are each made of **one / two** atoms; they are **monatomic / diatomic**.
- Halogens react with **metal / non-metal** elements to form crystalline compounds that are salts.
- The halogens get **more / less** reactive going down the group in the Periodic Table.
- Halogens can **colour / bleach** vegetable dyes and kill bacteria.

**e** Elements within a group tend to show clear trends in their physical properties as you go down a group. The following solid elements in Group VI show this. Complete the table by filling in the gaps. Use the following values when filling in the missing values.

685             4.79             0.198             450             0.221

| Name of element | sulfur | selenium | tellurium |
|---|---|---|---|
| density / g/cm³ | 2.07 | ............... | 6.24 |
| melting point / °C | 115 | 221 | ............... |
| boiling point / °C | 445 | ............... | 988 |
| ionic radius / nm | 0.184 | ............... | ............... |

# Exercise 3.2   The first four periods

> This exercise is aimed at developing your knowledge of the basic features of the Periodic Table and the properties of an element that relate to its position in the table.

The diagram below shows the upper part of the Periodic Table with certain elements selected.

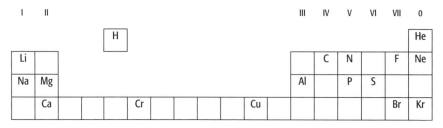

Using the elements shown above, write down the symbols for the elements which answer the following questions.

**a**   Which **two** elements are stored under oil because they are very reactive?

.......................................................................................................................................................................

**b**   Which **two** elements are transition metals?

.......................................................................................................................................................................

**c**   Which element has just two electrons in the full outer shell of its atom?

.......................................................................................................................................................................

**d**   Which element is a red-brown liquid at room temperature and pressure?

.......................................................................................................................................................................

**e**   Which element has four electrons in the outer energy level of its atom?

.......................................................................................................................................................................

**f**   Which element is a yellow solid at room temperature?

.......................................................................................................................................................................

**g**   Which elements are noble gases?

.......................................................................................................................................................................

**h**   Which element has compounds that produce blue solutions when they dissolve?

.......................................................................................................................................................................

**i**   Which element has the electron arrangement 2.8.8.2?

.......................................................................................................................................................................

**j**   Which element burns with a brilliant white flame when ignited?

.......................................................................................................................................................................

# Exercise 3.3   Trends in the halogens

> This exercise examines the trends in physical properties of elements within a non-metal group of the Periodic Table. It should help you develop your skills at analysing and predicting trends within a group.

The table shows some of the physical properties of the elements of Group VII at atmospheric pressure. These elements are known as the halogens and the properties show distinct trends as you go down the group.

| Element | Proton number | Melting point / °C | Boiling point / °C | Colour |
|---------|---------------|--------------------|--------------------|--------|
| fluorine | 9 | −219 | −188 | pale yellow |
| chlorine | 17 | −101 | −34 | pale green |
| bromine | 35 | −6 | | |
| iodine | 53 | 114 | 185 | grey-black |
| astatine | 85 | 303 | 337 | |

**a** Plot a graph of the melting points and boiling points of the halogens against their proton numbers. Join the points for each property together to produce two separate lines on the graph.

Draw a line across the graph at 20 °C (room temperature) to help you decide which elements are solid, liquid or gas at room temperature and pressure.

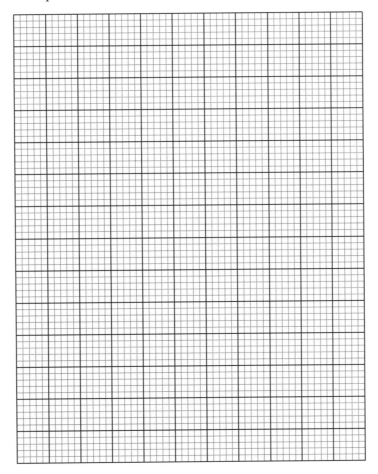

**b** Use your graph to estimate the boiling point of bromine, and state its colour and physical state at room temperature.

Estimated boiling point: ............................ °C          Colour: ..........................................................

Physical state: .......................................................

**c** Which of the halogens are gases at room temperature and pressure?

...........................................................................................................................................................

**d** Astatine is very rarely seen. What would you predict to be its physical state and colour at room temperature and pressure?

...........................................................................................................................................................

**e** What is the trend observed in the melting points of the halogens as you go down the group?

...........................................................................................................................................................

# Exercise 3.4   The chemical bonding in simple molecules

This exercise will familiarise you with the structures of some simple covalent compounds and the methods we have for representing the structure and shape of their molecules.

**a** Many covalent compounds exist as simple molecules where the atoms are joined together with single or double bonds. A covalent bond, made up of a shared pair of electrons, is often represented by a short straight line. Complete the table by filling in the blank spaces.

| Name of compound | Formula | Drawing of structure | Molecular model |
|---|---|---|---|
| hydrogen chloride | .................... | H — Cl | |
| water | $H_2O$ | O ⁄ \ H   H | |
| ammonia | .................... | | |
| .................... | $CH_4$ | | |
| ethene | .................... | H \ ⁄ H C=C ⁄ \ H   H | |
| .................... | .................... | O=C=O | |

**s** **b** Silicon(IV) oxide is a very common compound in the crust of the Earth. It has a giant covalent structure similar to diamond. Summarise the features of the structure of silicon(IV) oxide (silica), as shown in the diagram, by completing the following statements.

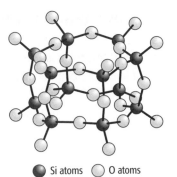

Si atoms ⚫    O atoms ⚪

- The strong bonds between the atoms

  are ..................................... bonds.

- In the crystal, there are two oxygen atoms for every silicon

  atom, so the formula is ..................................... .

- The atoms of the lattice are organised in a ..................................... arrangement

  like diamond, with a silicon atom at the centre of each ..................................... .

- This is an example of a ..................................... structure.

- Each oxygen atom forms ..................................... covalent bonds.

- Each silicon atom forms ..................................... covalent bonds.

**c** Graphite is one of the crystalline forms of carbon. Two of the distinctive properties of graphite are:

- it conducts electricity even though it is a non-metal, and
- it can act as a lubricant even though it has a giant covalent structure.

Give a brief explanation of these properties in the light of the structure of graphite.

**i** Graphite as an electrical conductor

...........................................................................................................................................................

...........................................................................................................................................................

...........................................................................................................................................................

**ii** Graphite as a lubricant

...........................................................................................................................................................

...........................................................................................................................................................

...........................................................................................................................................................

# Exercise 3.5  Formulae of ionic compounds

> The writing of chemical formulae is central to chemistry. This exercise will help you understand how to work out the formulae of ionic compounds and what such formulae mean.

The table below shows the valencies and formulae of some common ions.

| | | Valency | | |
|---|---|---|---|---|
| | | 1 | 2 | 3 |
| Positive ions (cations) | metals | sodium ($Na^+$) potassium ($K^+$) silver ($Ag^+$) | magnesium ($Mg^{2+}$) copper ($Cu^{2+}$) zinc ($Zn^{2+}$) iron ($Fe^{2+}$) | aluminium ($Al^{3+}$) iron ($Fe^{3+}$) chromium ($Cr^{3+}$) |
| | compound ions | ammonium ($NH_4^+$) | | |
| Negative ions (anions) | non-metals | chloride ($Cl^-$) bromide ($Br^-$) iodide ($I^-$) | oxide ($O^{2-}$) sulfide ($S^{2-}$) | nitride ($N^{3-}$) |
| | compound ions | nitrate ($NO_3^-$) hydroxide ($OH^-$) | carbonate ($CO_3^{2-}$) sulfate ($SO_4^{2-}$) | phosphate ($PO_4^{3-}$) |

a   Use the information in the table to work out the formulae of the following ionic compounds.

  i   Copper oxide                    .....................................

  ii   Sodium carbonate              .....................................

  iii   Zinc sulfate                  .....................................

  iv   Silver nitrate                 .....................................

  v   Magnesium bromide            .....................................

  vi   Ammonium sulfate             .....................................

  vii   Magnesium nitride            .....................................

  viii   Potassium phosphate         .....................................

  ix   Iron(III) hydroxide           .....................................

  x   Chromium(III) chloride        .....................................

b   Use the information in the table and your answers in **a** above to give the ratio of the different atoms in the following compounds.

  i   Copper oxide          Cu : O          .....................................

  ii   Magnesium bromide     Mg : Br         .....................................

  iii   Magnesium nitride     Mg : N          .....................................

  iv   Iron(III) hydroxide   Fe : O : H      .....................................

  v   Ammonium sulfate      N : H : S : O    .....................................

**c** The diagram below shows a representation of the structure of an ionic oxide.

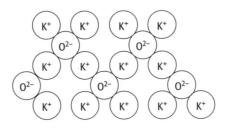

**i** What is the ratio of K⁺ ions to O²⁻ ions? .....................................

**ii** What is the formula of this compound? .....................................

**d** The following diagram shows the structure of common salt.
   **i** Extend the structure to the right, by adding **four** more ions.

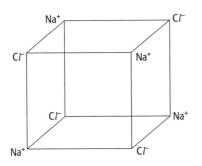

**ii** Complete the diagrams below for the ions in the structure to show their electron arrangement. Draw in any missing electron shells, showing clearly the origin of the electrons involved.

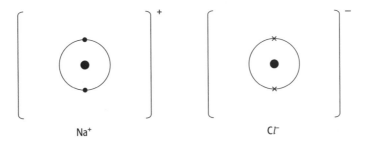

**iii** Draw an ionic diagram similar to the one above for the structure of magnesium chloride.

# Exercise 3.6   The bonding in covalent molecules

> The representation of the structures of covalent molecules is another important feature of chemistry. This exercise helps you develop your understanding of such structures and how to draw dot-and-cross diagrams of the sharing of electrons in these compounds.

Draw dot-and-cross and structural diagrams to represent the bonding in the following simple molecular compounds. In the dot-and-cross diagrams, show only the outer shells of the atoms involved.

| Molecule | Dot-and-cross diagram | Structure |
|---|---|---|
| Ammonia ($NH_3$) | | |
| Water ($H_2O$) | | |
| Hydrogen chloride (HCl) | | |
| Ethane ($C_2H_6$) | | |
| Ethene ($C_2H_4$) | Ⓢ | |

| Ethanol ($C_2H_5OH$) | | |
|---|---|---|
| Ethanoic acid ($CH_3COOH$) | | |

# Ⓢ Exercise 3.7   The nature of ionic lattices

> This exercise will help you relate the structures of ionic compounds to some of their key properties.

The diagram shows a model of the structure of sodium chloride and similar ionic crystals. The ions are arranged in a regular lattice structure – a giant ionic lattice.

The boxes below contain properties of ionic compounds and their explanations. Draw lines to link each pair.

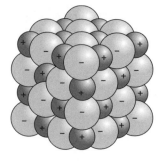

### Property

The solution of an ionic compound in water is a good conductor of electricity – such ionic substances are electrolytes.

Ionic crystals have a regular shape. All the crystals of each solid ionic compound are the same shape. Whatever the size of the crystal, the angles between the faces of the crystal are always the same.

Ionic compounds have relatively high melting points.

When an ionic compound is heated above its melting point, the molten compound is a good conductor of electricity.

### Explanation

The ions in the giant ionic structure are always arranged in the same regular way – see the diagram.

The giant ionic structure is held together by the strong attraction between the positive and negative ions. It takes a lot of energy to break down the regular arrangement of ions.

In a molten ionic compound, the positive and negative ions can move around – they can move to the electrodes when a voltage is applied.

In a solution of an ionic compound, the positive metal ions and the negative non-metal ions can move around – they can move to the electrodes when a voltage is applied.

# Exercise 3.8 Giant molecular lattices

> There are covalent substances where the bonding extends throughout the crystal. This exercise considers three major macromolecular structures and how their properties relate to their structure.

Sand is a powder of silicon(IV) oxide (sometimes called silica or silicon dioxide). Its structure is shown in the diagram.

silica

**a** Complete the following statements about the structure of silicon(IV) oxide by crossing out the incorrect bold words.

Silicon(IV) oxide occurs naturally as **mud / sand**. It has a giant **covalent / electrostatic** structure very similar to **graphite / diamond**. Such a structure can also be described as a **micromolecule / macromolecule** as all the atoms in the crystal are joined together by covalent bonds.

Each silicon atom is bonded to **four / two** oxygen atoms, while each oxygen atom is linked covalently to **four / two** silicon atoms. The oxygen atoms are arranged **hexagonally / tetrahedrally** around the silicon atoms.

The fact that all the atoms are bonded together in a **two-dimensional / three-dimensional** structure like **graphite / diamond** means that silicon(IV) oxide has similar physical properties to **graphite / diamond**. Silica is **very hard / slippery** and has a **low / high** melting point. All the outer electrons of the atoms in the structure are used in making the covalent bonds between the atoms. This means that silicon(IV) oxide **does / does not** conduct electricity. There are no electrons free to carry the current through the crystal.

**b** Below is a table of observations and explanations for diamond, graphite and silica. Complete the table by filling in the gaps. The first section of the table has been completed for you; other sections are only partly complete.

| Observation | Explanation |
|---|---|
| Diamond and silica are both very hard substances . . . | . . . because all the atoms in the structure are joined by strong covalent bonds |
| Diamond does not conduct electricity . . . | . . . because |
| Graphite is . . . | . . . because the layers in the structure are only held together by weak forces |
| | . . . because there are some free electrons that are able to move between the layers to carry the current |

# Exercise 3.9  Making magnesium oxide – a quantitative investigation

> This exercise will develop your skills in processing and interpreting results from practical work.

Magnesium oxide is made when magnesium is burnt in air. How does the mass of magnesium oxide made depend on the mass of magnesium burnt? The practical method is described below.

## Method

- Weigh an empty crucible and lid.
- Roll some magnesium ribbon round a pencil, place it in the crucible and re-weigh (not forgetting the lid).
- Place the crucible in a pipeclay triangle sitting safely on a tripod. (The lid should be on the crucible.)
- Heat the crucible and contents strongly, occasionally lifting the lid to allow more air in.
- When the reaction has eased, take off the lid.
- Heat strongly for another three minutes.
- Let the crucible cool down and then weigh it.
- Repeat the heating until the mass is constant.

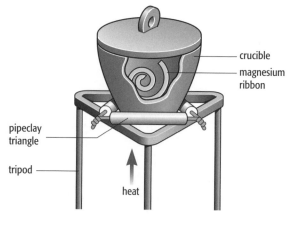

## Results

The table shows a set of class results calculated from the weights each student group obtained using this method.

| Mass of magnesium / g | 0.06 | 0.05 | 0.04 | 0.18 | 0.16 | 0.10 | 0.11 | 0.14 | 0.15 | 0.14 | 0.08 | 0.10 | 0.13 |
|---|---|---|---|---|---|---|---|---|---|---|---|---|---|
| Mass of magnesium oxide / g | 0.10 | 0.08 | 0.06 | 0.28 | 0.25 | 0.15 | 0.15 | 0.21 | 0.24 | 0.23 | 0.13 | 0.17 | 0.21 |

Use these results to plot a graph on the grid below relating mass of magnesium oxide made to mass of magnesium used. Remember there is one point on this graph that you can be certain of – what point is that? Include it on your graph.

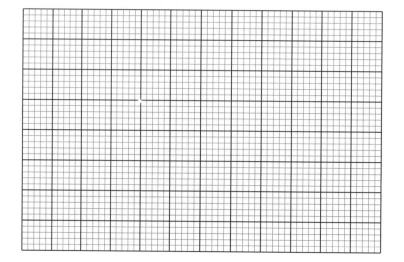

Use the checklist below to give yourself a mark for your graph.
For each point, award yourself:
2 marks if you did it really well
1 mark if you made a good attempt at it, and partly succeeded
0 marks if you did not try to do it, or did not succeed.

**Self-assessment checklist for graphs:**

| Check point | Marks awarded | |
| --- | --- | --- |
| | You | Your teacher |
| You have drawn the axes with a ruler, using most of the width and height of the grid. | | |
| You have used a good scale for the $x$-axis and the $y$-axis, going up in 0.01s, 0.05s or 0.10s. | | |
| You have labelled the axes correctly, giving the correct units for the scales on both axes. | | |
| You have plotted each point precisely and correctly. | | |
| You have used a small, neat cross for each point. | | |
| You have drawn a single, clear best-fit line through the points – using a ruler for a straight line. | | |
| You have ignored any anomalous results when drawing the line. | | |
| Total (out of 14) | | |

12–14  Excellent.
10–11  Good.
7–9    A good start, but you need to improve quite a bit.
5–6    Poor. Try this same graph again, using a new sheet of graph paper.
1–4    Very poor. Read through all the criteria again, and then try the same graph again.

a  How does the mass of magnesium oxide depend on the starting mass of magnesium?

......................................................................................................................................................

b  Work out from the graph the mass of magnesium oxide that you would get from 0.12 g of magnesium (show the

lines you use for this on your graph). ..................................... g

c  What mass of oxygen combines with 0.12 g of magnesium? ..................................... g

d  What mass of oxygen combines with 24 g of magnesium? ..................................... g

**S**  e  What is the formula of magnesium oxide, worked out on the basis of these results?
(Relative atomic masses: Mg = 24, O = 16.)

......................................................................................................................................................

......................................................................................................................................................

# 4 Chemical reactions

## Definitions to learn

- **synthesis**  the formation of a more complex compound from its elements (or simple substances)
- **decomposition**  the breakdown of a compound into simpler substances
- **precipitation**  the sudden formation of a solid during a chemical reaction
- **oxidation**  the addition of oxygen to an element or compound
- **reduction**  the removal of oxygen from a compound
- **electrolysis**  the decomposition (breakdown) of an ionic compound by the passage of an electric current
- **electrolyte**  a compound which conducts electricity when molten or in solution in water and is decomposed in the process
- **combustion**  the burning of an element or compound in air or oxygen
- **displacement**  a reaction in which a more reactive element displaces a less reactive element from a solution of a salt

## Useful reactions and their equations

copper carbonate $\rightarrow$ copper oxide + carbon dioxide

$$CuCO_3(s) \quad \rightarrow \quad CuO(s) \quad + \quad CO_2(g)$$  thermal decomposition

magnesium + oxygen $\rightarrow$ magnesium oxide

$$2Mg(s) \quad + \quad O_2(g) \rightarrow \quad 2MgO(s)$$  synthesis (oxidation)

copper oxide + hydrogen $\rightarrow$ copper + water

$$CuO(s) \quad + \quad H_2(g) \quad \rightarrow Cu(s) \; + H_2O(l)$$  reduction

methane + oxygen $\rightarrow$ carbon dioxide + water

$$CH_4(g) \quad + \quad O_2(g) \quad \rightarrow \quad CO_2(g) \quad + 2H_2O(l)$$  combustion

potassium iodide + chlorine $\rightarrow$ potassium chloride + iodine

$$2KI(aq) \quad + \quad Cl_2(g) \rightarrow \quad 2KCl(aq) \quad + I_2(aq)$$  displacement

copper(II) sulfate + zinc $\rightarrow$ zinc sulfate + copper

$$CuSO_4(aq) \quad + Zn(s) \rightarrow ZnSO_4(aq) + Cu(s)$$  displacement

# Exercise 4.1 Key chemical reactions

This exercise is designed to support your understanding of the basic aspects of some important types of chemical reaction.

**a** Complete the diagrams to show what substances are used and what is produced in burning, respiration and rusting.

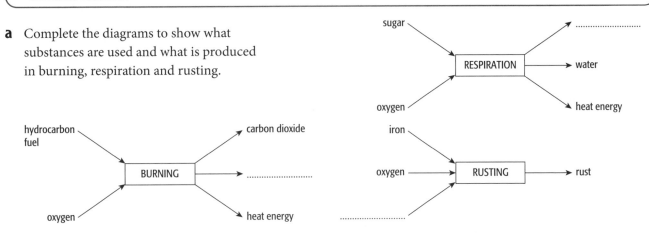

**b** What type of chemical change is involved in all of the above reactions? .....................................

**c** Oxidation and reduction reactions are important. There are several definitions of oxidation and reduction. Complete the following statements.

- If a substance **gains** oxygen during a reaction, it is ...................................... .
- If a substance ...................................... oxygen during a reaction, it is **reduced.**

**d** The diagram shows **A** the oxidation of copper to copper(II) oxide and **B** the reduction of copper oxide back to copper using hydrogen.

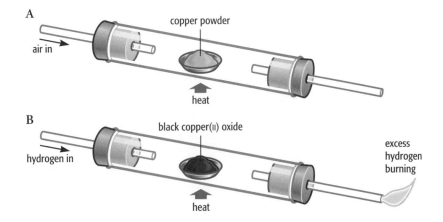

**i** Fill in the boxes on the equation below with the appropriate terms.

copper(II) oxide + hydrogen $\xrightarrow{\text{heat}}$ copper + water

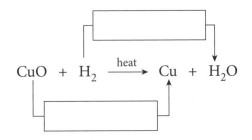

$$CuO \ + \ H_2 \ \xrightarrow{\text{heat}} \ Cu \ + \ H_2O$$

**ii** What type of agent is hydrogen acting as in this reaction? .....................................

**REMEMBER OIL RIG**

**e** A further definition links oxidation and reduction to the exchange of electrons during a reaction.

**i** Complete the following statements.

- Oxidation is the ..................................... of electrons.
- Reduction is the ..................................... of electrons.

**ii** Fill in the boxes on the ionic equation below with the appropriate terms.

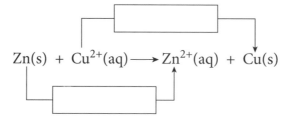

$$Zn(s) \ + \ Cu^{2+}(aq) \longrightarrow Zn^{2+}(aq) \ + \ Cu(s)$$

**iii** What type of agent are copper(II) ions acting as in this reaction? .....................................

# Exercise 4.2   The action of heat on metal carbonates

> This exercise will help you recall one of the major types of chemical reaction and help develop your skill at deducing conclusions from practical work.

The carbonates of many metallic elements decompose when heated.

**a** What type of reaction is this?

.................................................................................................................................................

**b** Name the gas produced during the breakdown of a metal carbonate, and describe a chemical test for this gas.

.................................................................................................................................................

.................................................................................................................................................

**c** A student investigates the breakdown of five different metal carbonates using the apparatus shown.

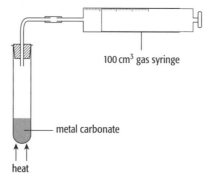

100 cm³ gas syringe

metal carbonate

heat

She heats a 0.010 mol sample of each carbonate using the blue flame of the same Bunsen burner. She measures the time it takes for 100 cm³ of gas to be collected in the gas syringe. The following table shows her results.

| Carbonate | Time taken to collect 100 cm³ of gas / s |
|---|---|
| metal A carbonate | 20 |
| metal B carbonate | 105 |
| metal C carbonate | 320 |
| metal D carbonate | no gas produced after 1000 |
| metal E carbonate | 60 |

In fact, the student used samples of calcium carbonate, copper(II) carbonate, magnesium carbonate, sodium carbonate and zinc carbonate.

Given the information that the more reactive a metal is, the less easy it is to break down the metal carbonate, complete the table to show the identity of each metal A, B, C, D and E.

| Metal | Name of metal |
|---|---|
| A | .................................... |
| B | .................................... |
| C | .................................... |
| D | .................................... |
| E | .................................... |

**d** Write the chemical equation for the breakdown of zinc carbonate.

.....................................................................................................................................................................................

# Exercise 4.3   The nature of electrolysis

> This exercise will help you summarise the major aspects of electrolysis and its applications.

**a** Complete the following passage by using the words listed below.

anode        electrodes      current       molten      electrolyte     solution     cathode
positive      hydrogen        molecules     lose        oxygen

## Changes taking place during electrolysis

During electrolysis ionic compounds are decomposed by the passage of an electric current. For this to happen, the

compound must be either ................................... or in .................................... . Electrolysis can occur when an

electric ................................... passes through a molten .................................... . The two rods dipping into the

electrolyte are called the .................................... . In this situation, metals are deposited at the

................................... and non-metals are formed at the .................................... .

When the ionic compound is dissolved in water, the electrolysis can be more complex. Generally, during electrolysis

................................... ions move towards the .................................... and negative ions move towards the

................................... . At the negative electrode (cathode) the metal or .................................... ions gain

electrons and form metal atoms or hydrogen .................................... . At the positive electrode (anode) certain

non-metal ions ................................... electrons and .................................... or chlorine is produced.

**b** Complete the passage by using the words listed below.

hydrogen    hydroxide    lower    copper    sodium    molten
cryolite    purifying    positive    concentrated

### Examples of electrolysis in industry

There are several important industrial applications of electrolysis, the most important economically being the

electrolysis of ................................. aluminium oxide to produce aluminium. The aluminium oxide is mixed with

molten ................................. to ................................. the melting point of the electrolyte.

A ................................. aqueous solution of sodium chloride contains ................................., chloride,

hydrogen and ................................. ions. When this solution is electrolysed, ................................. rather than

sodium is discharged at the negative electrode. The solution remaining is sodium hydroxide.

When a solution of copper(II) sulfate is electrolysed using ................................. electrodes, an unusual thing

happens and the copper atoms of the ................................. electrode (anode) go into solution as copper ions. At

the cathode the copper ions turn into copper atoms, and the metal is deposited on this electrode. This can be used as

a method of refining or ................................. impure copper.

# Exercise 4.4    Displacement reactions of the halogens

> This exercise will build your understanding of a certain type of reaction and help improve your skills in organising and presenting experimental observations.

The halogens – chlorine, bromine and iodine – differ in terms of their ability to displace another halogen from a solution of its salt. The following are some notes from a students experiment. They include some rough observations from the tests carried out.

The halogens were provided as solutions in water and the test was to add the halogen to the salt solution. Solutions of potassium chloride, potassium bromide and potassium iodide were provided.

To add further observations, hexane was also available as a solvent to mix with the reaction mixture at the end of the experiment. If there appeared to be a reaction, the product was shaken with hexane and the layers allowed to separate. The colour, if any, of the hexane layer was noted.

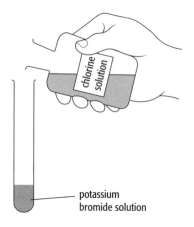

chlorine solution

potassium bromide solution

## Results

1  Rough notes: KCl solution with bromine or iodine solutions – no change to colourless solution – hexane not added.

2  KBr solution with iodine solution – no change to colourless solution – hexane not added.

3  KBr solution with chlorine solution – solution colourless to brown – brown colour moves to upper hexane layer at end.

4  KI solution with chlorine or bromine water – solution colourless to brown in both cases – purple colour in upper hexane layer at end (brown colour of aqueous layer reduced).

a  Take these recorded observations and draw up a table of the results. If there is no change, then write 'no reaction'.

Use this checklist to give yourself a mark for your results table.

For each point, award yourself:

2 marks if you did it really well

1 mark if you made a good attempt at it, and partly succeeded

0 marks if you did not try to do it, or did not succeed.

**Self-assessment checklist for results tables:**

| Check point | Marks awarded | |
|---|---|---|
| | You | Your teacher |
| You have drawn the table with a ruler. | | |
| The headings are appropriate and cover the observations you expect to make. | | |
| The observations are recorded accurately, clearly and concisely – without over-elaboration. | | |
| The table is easy for someone else to read and understand. | | |
| Total (out of 8) | | |

8     Excellent.

7     Good.

5–6   A good start, but you need to improve quite a bit.

3–4   Poor. Try this same results table again, using a new sheet of paper.

1–2   Very poor. Read through all the criteria again, and then try the same results table again.

**b**   Use the results to complete the diagram below which places the halogens tested in order of increasing reactivity.

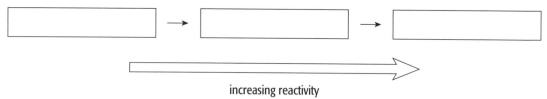

increasing reactivity

# Exercise 4.5   Self-heating cans, hand warmers and cool packs

Chemical reactions involve energy changes and this fact can be exploited for a range of practical purposes. This exercise illustrates those purposes and introduces aspects of exothermic and endothermic reactions which will also be met in later chapters.

## Self-heating cans

Drinks, soups and other foods can be purchased in self-heating cans. Such containers are particularly useful on expeditions and in circumstances where transportation space is restricted.

These cans rely on a chemical reaction that produces sufficient heat to raise the temperature of the drink or food that surrounds the reaction vessel. The most common reaction used is the reaction between calcium oxide (slaked lime) and water. When this reaction takes place, a great deal of heat is given off and the solid calcium oxide swells to occupy a greater volume.

The diagram shows one way in which such a can may be constructed.

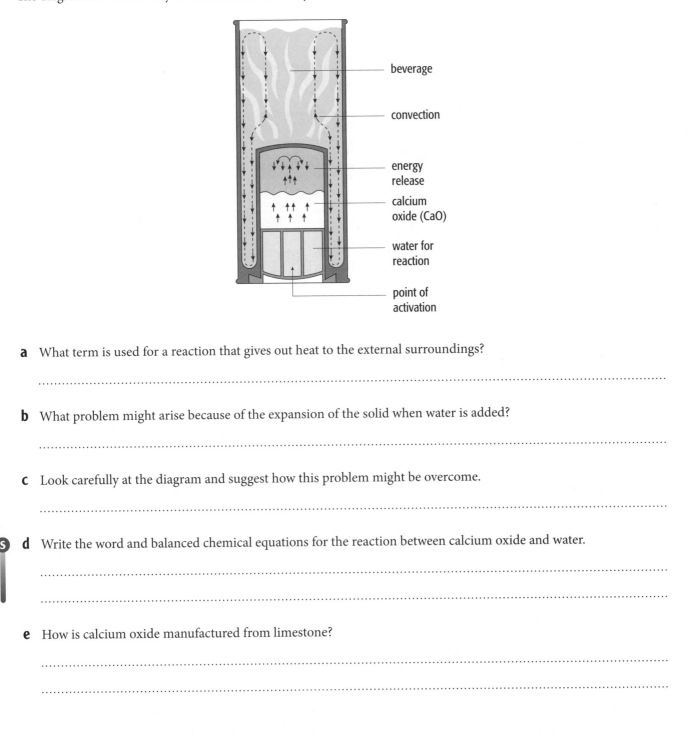

a  What term is used for a reaction that gives out heat to the external surroundings?

.......................................................................................................................................................................

b  What problem might arise because of the expansion of the solid when water is added?

.......................................................................................................................................................................

c  Look carefully at the diagram and suggest how this problem might be overcome.

.......................................................................................................................................................................

**S**  d  Write the word and balanced chemical equations for the reaction between calcium oxide and water.

.......................................................................................................................................................................

.......................................................................................................................................................................

e  How is calcium oxide manufactured from limestone?

.......................................................................................................................................................................

.......................................................................................................................................................................

**f** Using the internet, find **two** other exothermic reactions that are used in self-heating cans.

.................................................................................................................................

.................................................................................................................................

## Heat pads and hand warmers

Some reactions are not obviously exothermic but have uses in this context. For example, the rusting reaction of iron generates heat for several hours and is used in pocket hand warmers for expeditions to cold regions. It is also used in the heat pads employed in first aid to relieve the aches and pains caused by strain in muscles and joints.

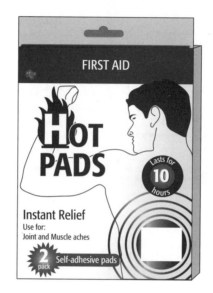

**a** The heat pad contains iron powder and water absorbed within the pad. While sealed, the rusting reaction cannot take place. What further reactant is needed which only comes into play when the sealed packaging is opened?

.................................................................................................................................

**b** Rust is hydrated iron(III) oxide. What is the chemical formula of iron(III) oxide?

.................................................................................................................................

**c** Complete the equation for the formation of rust.

$$........ Fe + ........ O_2 + 2xH_2O \rightarrow ........ Fe_2O_3 \cdot xH_2O$$

**d** The pad also contains salt. Why is this present as a component of the reacting mixture?

.................................................................................................................................

.................................................................................................................................

**e** Hand warmers can be made using a solution of sodium thiosulfate which contains more than the normal amount of the salt that can be dissolved at room temperature. A metallic 'clicker' is used to create a physical disturbance in the solution and the excess salt crystallises out, releasing a substantial amount of heat.

**i** What is the term used for such a solution that contains more dissolved solute than is normal?

.................................................................................................................................................

**ii** How can such a hand warmer be re-used after the salt has been crystallised out?

.................................................................................................................................................

.................................................................................................................................................

**iii** Is a hand warmer based on the rusting reaction re-usable? Explain your answer.

.................................................................................................................................................

.................................................................................................................................................

## Cool packs

Reactions that absorb heat from the surroundings are also of use in circumstances where things needed to be cooled down or kept cool. There are two types of cool pack:

- instant cool packs that contain a solid which dissolves endothermically in water that is kept separate from the solid in the package until needed
- cool packs that contain a gel which is cooled down in a freezer and which warms up slowly when removed. This type of cool pack can be re-used.

Instant cool packs usually contain crystals of ammonium nitrate together with a plastic bag of water which is burst to activate the pack.

**a** Give another use for ammonium nitrate.

.................................................................................................................................................

**b** Give **one** advantage and **one** disadvantage of this type of cool pack.

Advantage:

.................................................................................................................................................

Disadvantage:

.................................................................................................................................................

c   Cool packs can be used to keep vaccines and other medicines cool in hot climates. A temperature of 5 °C is usually required. Devise an experiment to discover how much ammonium nitrate and how much water would have to be used to produce the temperature of 5 °C needed to keep a vaccine cool in hot desert conditions.

.......................................................................................................................................................................................

.......................................................................................................................................................................................

.......................................................................................................................................................................................

.......................................................................................................................................................................................

.......................................................................................................................................................................................

# Exercise 4.6   The movement of ions

> **This exercise introduces the idea of the movement of ions in an electrical field and the basis of the terms anion and cation.**

A student set up an experiment like this to look at the movement of ions. The filter paper is damp and a small crystal of the solid being studied is placed in the centre as shown.

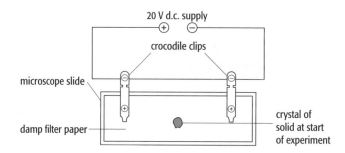

The results are shown in the table.

| Substance | Colour of crystals | Changes seen on the filter paper |
|---|---|---|
| potassium chromate, $K_2CrO_4$ | yellow | yellow colour moves towards positive |
| potassium sulfate, $K_2SO_4$ | white | no colours seen |
| copper sulfate, $CuSO_4$ | blue | blue colour moves towards negative |

a   Which of these ions is yellow?

chromate          copper          potassium          sulfate

.......................................................................................................................................................................................

**b** Explain why the yellow colour moves towards the positive terminal in the potassium chromate experiment.

..................................................................................................................................................................

..................................................................................................................................................................

**c** List the anions and cations involved in this experiment, together with their formulae.

Anions:

..................................................................................................................................................................

Cations:

..................................................................................................................................................................

**d** Suggest and explain what will happen if this experiment is repeated with copper chromate.

..................................................................................................................................................................

..................................................................................................................................................................

..................................................................................................................................................................

..................................................................................................................................................................

# Exercise 4.7 Making and 'breaking' copper chloride

> The difference between synthesis and decomposition is emphasised in this exercise together with a consideration of the energy changes involved.

'Dutch metal' is a form of brass containing a very high proportion of copper. It is generally used as very thin sheets for gilding, as imitation gold leaf.

## Synthesising copper(II) chloride

**a** What are the words we use to describe a metal that can be drawn out and beaten into thin sheets?

.....................................................................................................................................................

The following is a description of the reaction of Dutch metal with chlorine gas to produce copper(II) chloride.

*A clean dry gas jar is filled with chlorine gas in a fume cupboard. The lid of the gas jar is lifted and two thin sheets of Dutch metal are lowered into the gas using tongs. The lid is quickly replaced.*

*A flash of flame is observed and clouds of yellow 'smoke' are formed.*

*A small volume of distilled water is added to the gas jar and shaken to dissolve the smoke. A pale blue-green (turquoise) solution is formed.*

**b** What colour is chlorine gas?

.....................................................................................................................................................

**c** Why is the reaction carried out in a fume cupboard?

.....................................................................................................................................................

**d** Is the reaction observed exothermic or endothermic? What feature of Dutch metal helps the reaction take place quickly? Explain your answers.

.....................................................................................................................................................

.....................................................................................................................................................

.....................................................................................................................................................

**e** What observation indicates that the solution obtained contains copper(II) chloride?

.....................................................................................................................................................

**f** Give the chemical equation for the synthesis reaction that has taken place.

.....................................................................................................................................................

**g** Dutch metal is an alloy of copper (84%) and zinc (16%). What other salt may be present in the solution?

.....................................................................................................................................................

## Decomposing copper(II) chloride

Copper(II) chloride can be decomposed to its elements by electrolysis. A simple cell such as the one shown here can be set up so that the chlorine gas can be collected.

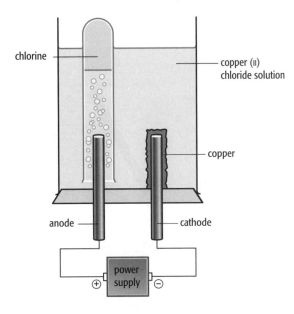

**a**  Write word and symbol equations for the overall reaction taking place during this electrolysis.

..................................................................................................................................................

..................................................................................................................................................

**b**  Define the term **electrolysis**.

..................................................................................................................................................

..................................................................................................................................................

..................................................................................................................................................

..................................................................................................................................................

**c**  How would you test the gas collected at the anode to show that it was chlorine?

..................................................................................................................................................

..................................................................................................................................................

**d** A much simpler set of apparatus can be used to show this electrolysis. This is shown below.

**i** If this simpler apparatus is used, where must the electrolysis be carried out for safety reasons?

.......................................................................................................................................................................

**ii** Using this simple apparatus, there is no collection of any gas produced. How could you test to show that chlorine had been produced in this case? Explain why it would work.

.......................................................................................................................................................................

.......................................................................................................................................................................

.......................................................................................................................................................................

**e** Is the decomposition of copper(II) chloride exothermic or endothermic? What type of energy is involved in this reaction?

.......................................................................................................................................................................

.......................................................................................................................................................................

**f** Write the half-equations for the reactions taking place at the anode (positive electrode) and the cathode (negative electrode).

At the anode:

.......................................................................................................................................................................

At the cathode:

.......................................................................................................................................................................

# 5 Acids, bases and salts

## Definitions to learn

- **acid** a substance that dissolves in water to give a solution with a pH below 7
- **base** a substance which will neutralise an acid to give a salt and water only
- **alkali** a base that dissolves in water
- **pH scale** a measure of the acidity or alkalinity of a solution (scale from 0 to 14)
- **indicator** a substance that changes colour depending on whether it is in an acid or alkali
- **salt** an ionic substance produced from an acid by neutralisation with a base
- **neutralisation reaction** a reaction between an acid and a base to produce a salt and water only

## Useful reactions and their equations

**Neutralisation reactions**

$HCl(aq) + NaOH(aq) \rightarrow NaCl(aq) + H_2O(l)$

$H_2SO_4(aq) + 2KOH(aq) \rightarrow K_2SO_4(aq) + 2H_2O(l)$

$HNO_3(aq) + NH_3(aq) \rightarrow NH_4NO_3(aq)$

$CuO(s) + H_2SO_4(aq) \rightarrow CuSO_4(aq) + H_2O(l)$

**Other characteristic acid reactions**

$CaCO_3(s) + 2HCl(aq) \rightarrow CaCl_2(aq) + CO_2(g) + H_2O(l)$

$CuCO_3(s) + H_2SO_4(aq) \rightarrow CuSO_4(aq) + CO_2(g) + H_2O(l)$

$Zn(s) + H_2SO_4(aq) \rightarrow ZnSO_4(aq) + H_2(g)$

$Mg(s) + 2HCl(aq) \rightarrow MgCl_2(aq) + H_2(g)$

**Precipitation reactions**

$FeSO_4(aq) + 2NaOH(aq) \rightarrow Fe(OH)_2(s) + Na_2SO_4(aq)$

$AlCl_3(aq) + 3NaOH(aq) \rightarrow Al(OH)_3(s) + 3NaCl(aq)$

$AgNO_3(aq) + KI(aq) \rightarrow AgI(s) + KNO_3(aq)$

## Exercise 5.1   Acid and base reactions – neutralisation

> This exercise will help you familiarise yourself with some of the terms involved in talking about acids and bases.

Choose words from the list below to fill in the gaps in the following statements.

| | | | | |
|---|---|---|---|---|
| acid | carbon dioxide | hydrogen | hydrated | anhydrous |
| metal | precipitation | sodium | sulfuric | water |

All salts are **ionic** compounds. Salts are produced when an alkali neutralises an ........................................ .

In this reaction, the salt is formed when a ........................................ ion or an ammonium ion from the alkali

replaces one or more ........................................ ions of the acid.

Salts can be crystallised from the solution produced by the neutralisation reaction. The salt crystals formed often

contain ....................................... of crystallisation. These salts are called ....................................... salts.

The salt crystals can be heated to drive off the ....................................... of crystallisation. The salt remaining is

said to be ....................................... .

Salts can be made by other reactions of acids. Magnesium sulfate can be made by reacting magnesium carbonate

with ....................................... acid. The gas given off is ....................................... . Water is also formed in

this reaction.

All ....................................... salts are soluble in water. Insoluble salts are usually prepared

by ....................................... .

# Exercise 5.2   Types of salt

> This exercise aims to increase your confidence in predicting the products of the characteristic reactions of acids, particularly in terms of naming the salt produced in a reaction.

Salts are produced in reactions where the hydrogen of an acid is replaced by metal ions or the ammonium ion. Each acid gives a characteristic family of salts. Sulfuric acid, for instance, always produces sulfates.

**a**   Complete the following statements for other acids.

   **i**    Hydrochloric acid always produces ....................................... .

   **ii**   Nitric acid always produces ....................................... .

   **iii**  Ethanoic acid always produces ....................................... .

   **iv**  Phosphoric acid always produces ....................................... .

**b** Complete the table below which summarises the products of various reactions of acids.

| Substances reacted together | | Salt produced | Other products of the reaction |
|---|---|---|---|
| dilute hydrochloric acid | zinc oxide | | |
| dilute sulfuric acid | | copper sulfate | water and carbon dioxide |
| | | magnesium sulfate | water and carbon dioxide |
| | | magnesium chloride | hydrogen |
| dilute nitric acid | copper oxide | | |
| dilute ethanoic acid | | sodium ethanoate | water |
| | potassium hydroxide | potassium phosphate | |

# Exercise 5.3   Antacids

This exercise discusses the different compounds that we can use to counteract the effects of acid indigestion.
The reactions involved with the different remedies are considered.

The human stomach contains hydrochloric acid with a pH of about 2. This plays a part in the process by which we digest our food. Acid indigestion (heartburn) is due to the stomach producing too much hydrochloric acid. This causes discomfort and often pain.

One way to deal with this is to take an antacid. Antacids contain chemicals which react with and neutralise the acid in the stomach.

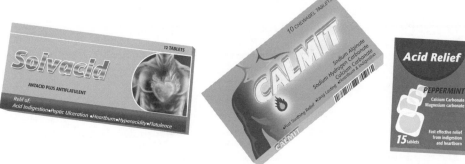

Below are listed a number of common ingredients of antacid remedies:

- sodium carbonate
- sodium hydrogencarbonate
- calcium carbonate
- magnesium carbonate
- magnesium hydroxide
- aluminium hydroxide
- sodium alginate.

**a** Write equations showing the reactions between magnesium carbonate and magnesium hydroxide with hydrochloric acid.

 **i** $MgCO_3$

 .......................................................................................................................................................

 **ii** $Mg(OH)_2$

 .......................................................................................................................................................

**b** Why might the reaction with magnesium carbonate cause some discomfort?

 .......................................................................................................................................................

**c** Some of the compounds listed earlier are soluble in water.

 **i** Which **two** compounds are soluble in water?

 .......................................................................................................................................................

 **ii** Why might these compounds work more quickly?

 .......................................................................................................................................................

 .......................................................................................................................................................

**d** Sodium alginate does not neutralise acid. Use the internet to find why it is used in antacids.

 .......................................................................................................................................................

 .......................................................................................................................................................

 .......................................................................................................................................................

## Ⓐ Exercise 5.4    Fire extinguishers

> Carbon dioxide is often used in fire extinguishers. This exercise describes a traditional 'wet' carbon dioxide extinguisher, and discusses the different types of extinguisher and their appropriate use. You can use the internet to research other types of fire extinguisher.

The diagram shows an early type of fire extinguisher. The extinguisher was turned upside down causing the stopper to come out of the acid bottle.

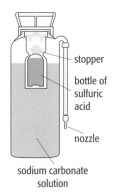

stopper

bottle of sulfuric acid

nozzle

sodium carbonate solution

The reaction between acid and carbonate then produced a mixture of water and carbon dioxide which was squirted at the fire. It was important that a large volume of carbon dioxide was produced quickly.

This type of extinguisher is not suitable for all types of fire.

It is possible to use sodium hydrogencarbonate instead of sodium carbonate and hydrochloric acid instead of sulfuric acid.

**a**   Below are the equations for the possible reactions:

**1**   $Na_2CO_3 + H_2SO_4 \rightarrow Na_2SO_4 + H_2O + CO_2$

**2**   $Na_2CO_3 + 2HCl \rightarrow 2NaCl + H_2O + CO_2$

**3**   $2NaHCO_3 + H_2SO_4 \rightarrow Na_2SO_4 + 2H_2O + 2CO_2$

**4**   $NaHCO_3 + HCl \rightarrow NaCl + H_2O + CO_2$

Answer the following questions, assuming that all four solutions are of the same concentration and in equal volumes.

**i**   Which combination(s) would produce carbon dioxide most quickly? Explain your answer.

.............................................................................................................................................................

.............................................................................................................................................................

.............................................................................................................................................................

**ii** Which combination(s) would produce least carbon dioxide? Explain your answer.

.......................................................................................................................................................

.......................................................................................................................................................

.......................................................................................................................................................

**A** **b** Use the internet to discover what types of fire extinguisher are used now. Comment on the type(s) of fire they are useful for and the types they are not.

.......................................................................................................................................................

.......................................................................................................................................................

.......................................................................................................................................................

.......................................................................................................................................................

.......................................................................................................................................................

.......................................................................................................................................................

**c** Which extinguisher is sometimes called the 'universal extinguisher' and why?

.......................................................................................................................................................

.......................................................................................................................................................

.......................................................................................................................................................

# Exercise 5.5   Descaling a coffee machine

> The formation of limescale in coffee makers, kettles and hot water pipes is a problem in certain areas. This exercise considers various acids that are used to remove limescale and their effectiveness.

Coffee makers can become blocked with 'limescale' in hard water areas. Limescale is calcium carbonate which precipitates from the hot water in the machine and blocks the pipes.

It is often necessary to 'descale' the machines. This is done by passing acid through the pipes. The acid reacts with the calcium carbonate and so removes it.

The following acids have been used for descaling:

- hydrochloric acid
- citric acid
- ethanoic acid (vinegar)
- sulfamic acid.

**a** Write word and symbol equations for the reaction between calcium carbonate and hydrochloric acid.

.................................................................................................................................................................

.................................................................................................................................................................

**b** What name would be given to the salt formed when citric acid reacts with calcium carbonate?

.................................................................................................................................................................

**c** Why might these acids not be the best to use for descaling a coffee machine?

  **i** Hydrochloric acid

.................................................................................................................................................................

  **ii** Ethanoic acid

.................................................................................................................................................................

**d** Search the internet to find the answers to the following questions.

  **i** What is the formula of sulfamic acid and what is it used for?

.................................................................................................................................................................

.................................................................................................................................................................

  **ii** Why does water sometimes produce calcium carbonate (limescale) when it is heated? What is hard water?

.................................................................................................................................................................

.................................................................................................................................................................

.................................................................................................................................................................

.................................................................................................................................................................

.................................................................................................................................................................

# Exercise 5.6　The analysis of titration results

> This exercise will develop your understanding of some of the practical skills involved in acid–base titrations and the processing and evaluation of experimental results.

A student investigated an aqueous solution of sodium hydroxide and its reaction with hydrochloric acid. He carried out two experiments.

## Experiment 1

Using a measuring cylinder, 10 cm³ of the sodium hydroxide solution was placed in a conical flask. Methyl orange indicator was added to the flask. A burette was filled to the 0.0 cm³ mark with hydrochloric acid (solution **P**).

The student added solution **P** slowly to the alkali in the flask until the colour just disappeared. Use the burette diagram to record the volume in the results table and then complete the column for experiment 1.

Experiment 1 Final reading

## Experiment 2

Experiment **1** was repeated using a different solution of hydrochloric acid (solution **Q**).

Use the burette diagrams to record the volumes in the results table and complete the column.

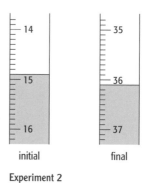

initial　　final

Experiment 2

## Table of results

| Burette readings / cm³ | Experiment 1 | Experiment 2 |
|---|---|---|
| final reading | ................... | ................... |
| initial reading | 0.0 | ................... |
| difference | ................... | ................... |

**a** What type of chemical reaction occurs when hydrochloric acid reacts with sodium hydroxide?

..............................................................................................................................................

**b** Write a word equation for the reaction.

..............................................................................................................................................

**c** What was the colour change of the indicator observed?

..............................................................................................................................................

**d** Which of the experiments used the greater volume of hydrochloric acid?

..............................................................................................................................................

**e** Compare the volumes of acid used in experiments **1** and **2** and suggest an explanation for the difference between the volumes.

..............................................................................................................................................

..............................................................................................................................................

**f** Predict the volume of hydrochloric acid **P** that would be needed to react completely if experiment **1** was repeated with 25 cm³ of sodium hydroxide solution.

Volume of solution needed: ......................................

Explanation

..............................................................................................................................................

**g** Suggest **one** change the student could make to the **apparatus** used in order to obtain more accurate results.

..............................................................................................................................................

# Exercise 5.7   Thermochemistry – investigating the neutralisation of an acid by an alkali

> This exercise introduces an unfamiliar form of titration and further develops your skills in presenting, processing and evaluating the results of practical work.

The reaction between dilute nitric acid and dilute sodium hydroxide solutions can be investigated by thermochemistry. This can be done by following the changes in temperature as one solution is added to another.

## Apparatus

- polystyrene cup and beaker
- 25 cm$^3$ measuring cylinder
- 100 cm$^3$ measuring cylinder
- thermometer (0 to 100 °C)
- **safety glasses – to be used when handling the acid and alkali solutions**

## Method

An experiment was carried out to measure the temperature changes during the neutralisation of sodium hydroxide solution with dilute nitric acid. Both solutions were allowed to stand in the laboratory for about 30 minutes.

25 cm$^3$ of sodium hydroxide solution was added to a polystyrene beaker and the temperature was measured. Then 10 cm$^3$ of nitric acid was added to the alkali in the beaker and the highest temperature reached was measured. The experiment was repeated using the following volumes of acid: 20, 30, 40, 50 and 60 cm$^3$.

## Results

Temperature of alkali solution at start of experiment = 21.0 °C.

The following temperatures were obtained for the different volumes of added acid used:

28.0, 35.0, 35.0, 31.0, 30.0 and 27.5 °C respectively.

**a**   Record these results here in a suitable table.

Use this checklist to give yourself a mark for your results table.

For each point, award yourself:

2 marks if you did it really well

1 mark if you made a good attempt at it, and partly succeeded

0 marks if you did not try to do it, or did not succeed.

**Self-assessment checklist for results tables:**

| Check point | Marks awarded | |
| --- | --- | --- |
| | You | Your teacher |
| You have drawn the table with a ruler. | | |
| The headings are appropriate and have the correct units in each column/row. | | |
| The table is easy for someone else to read and understand. | | |
| If the table contains readings, all are to the same number of decimal places (for example 15.5, 14.2, etc). | | |
| Total (out of 8) | | |

8   Excellent.

7   Good.

5–6   A good start, but you need to improve quite a bit.

3–4   Poor. Try this same results table again, using a new sheet of paper.

1–2   Very poor. Read through all the criteria again, and then try the same results table again.

**b** Plot a graph of the temperature of the solution against the volume of acid added to the alkali.

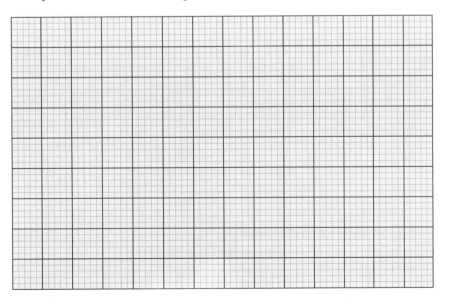

**c** Draw suitable lines through the points on your graph. (Note that there are two parts to this graph so you will need to draw **two** straight lines through the points and extend them until they cross.)

**d** Which point appears to be inaccurate?

.................................................................................................................................................................

**e** From these results work out the volume of acid needed to neutralise 25 cm³ of the sodium hydroxide solution. Explain why you have chosen this value.

.................................................................................................................................................................

.................................................................................................................................................................

Use the checklist below to give yourself a mark for your graph.
For each point, award yourself:
2 marks if you did it really well
1 mark if you made a good attempt at it, and partly succeeded
0 marks if you did not try to do it, or did not succeed.

**Self-assessment checklist for graphs:**

| Check point | Marks awarded | |
| --- | --- | --- |
| | **You** | **Your teacher** |
| You have drawn the axes with a ruler, using most of the width and height of the grid. | | |
| You have used a good scale for the x-axis and the y-axis, going up in 1s, 2s, 5s or 10s. | | |
| You have labelled the axes correctly, giving the correct units for the scales on both axes. | | |
| You have plotted each point precisely and correctly. | | |
| You have used a small, neat cross for each point. | | |
| You have drawn a single, clear best-fit line through each set of points – using a ruler for straight lines – and have extended the lines to meet. | | |
| You have ignored any anomalous results when drawing the lines. | | |
| **Total (out of 14)** | | |

12–14   Excellent.
10–11   Good.
7–9     A good start, but you need to improve quite a bit.
5–6     Poor. Try this same graph again, using a new sheet of graph paper.
1–4     Very poor. Read through all the criteria again, and then try the same graph again.

**f**  Why were the solutions left to stand for about 30 minutes before the experiments?

.......................................................................................................................................................................

**g**  Why was a polystyrene beaker used instead of a glass beaker?

.......................................................................................................................................................................

**h**  Suggest **three** improvements that would make the experiment more accurate.

.......................................................................................................................................................................

.......................................................................................................................................................................

.......................................................................................................................................................................

**i**  Write the word equation and balanced chemical equation for the reaction.

.......................................................................................................................................................................

.......................................................................................................................................................................

**j**  Is the reaction exothermic or endothermic? ....................................................................................................

**k**  The concentration of the sodium hydroxide solution is 1.0 mole per $dm^3$. How many moles are there in $25\,cm^3$ of this solution? (Remember there are $1000\,cm^3$ in $1\,dm^3$.)

.......................................................................................................................................................................

**l**  Look at the equation and work out how many moles of nitric acid this would react with.

.......................................................................................................................................................................

**m**  Calculate how many moles of acid there are in $1000\,cm^3$ of the acid solution. What is the concentration of the acid solution in moles per $dm^3$?

.......................................................................................................................................................................

# Exercise 5.8  Deducing a formula from a precipitation reaction

> This exercise will help you familiarise yourself with an unusual method of finding the formula of an insoluble salt using precipitation.

Insoluble salts can be made using a precipitation reaction. The method can be used to find the formula of a salt. In an experiment, $6.0\,cm^3$ of a solution of the nitrate of metal X was placed in a narrow test tube and $1.0\,cm^3$ of aqueous sodium phosphate, $Na_3PO_4$, was added. The precipitate settled and its height was measured.

The concentration of both solutions was $1.00\,mol/dm^3$.

The experiment was repeated using different volumes of the sodium phosphate solution. The results are shown on the graph.

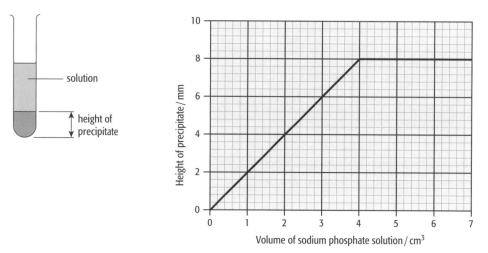

What is the formula of the phosphate of metal X? Give your reasoning.

..............................................................................................................................................................................

..............................................................................................................................................................................

..............................................................................................................................................................................

# 6 Quantitative chemistry

## Definitions to learn

- **relative atomic mass**  the average mass of naturally occurring atoms of an element on a scale where the carbon-12 atom has a mass of exactly 12 units
- **relative formula mass**  the sum of all the relative atomic masses of all the atoms or ions in a compound
- **empirical formula**  the formula of a compound that shows the simplest ratio of the atoms in a compound in whole numbers
- **mole**  the relative formula mass of a substance in grams
- **molar gas volume**  the volume occupied by one mole of any gas ($24\,dm^3$ at room temperature and pressure)

## Exercise 6.1   Calculating formula masses

This exercise will develop your understanding and recall of the ideas about atomic and formula mass.

**a**  Complete the following diagram by filling in the blanks.

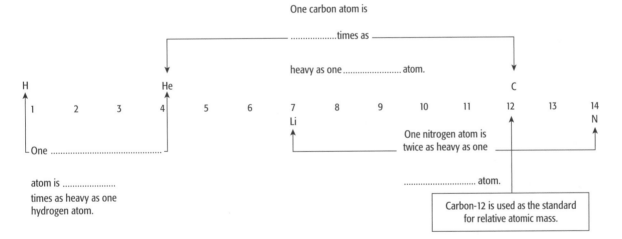

**b** Complete the following table of formula masses for a range of different types of substance.
(Relative atomic masses: O = 16, H = 1, C = 12, N = 14, Ca = 40, Mg = 24.)

| Molecule | Chemical formula | Number of atoms or ions involved | Relative formula mass |
|---|---|---|---|
| oxygen | $O_2$ | 2 O | $2 \times 16 = 32$ |
| carbon dioxide | .................... | 1 C and 2 O | $1 \times 12 + 2 \times 16 =$ .................... |
| .................... | $H_2O$ | 2 H and 1.................... | .................... = .................... |
| ammonia | .................... | 1 N and 3 H | .................... = .................... |
| calcium carbonate | .................... | 1 $Ca^{2+}$ and 1 $CO_3^{2-}$ | ........... + ........... $+ 3 \times 16 = 100$ |
| .................... | MgO | 1 $Mg^{2+}$ and 1 $O^{2-}$ | $1 \times 24 + 1 \times 16 =$ .......... |
| ammonium nitrate | $NH_4NO_3$ | 1 $NH_4^+$ and .................... | $2 \times 14 +$ .................... + .................... = 80 |
| propanol | $C_3H_7OH$ | 3 C, ........... and ......... | $3 \times 12 + 8 \times 1 +$ ........... = ........... |

# Exercise 6.2   A sense of proportion in chemistry

This exercise will familiarise you with some of the basic calculations involved in chemistry.

**a**   Zinc metal is extracted from its oxide. In the industrial extraction process, 5 tonnes of zinc oxide are needed to produce 4 tonnes of zinc. Calculate the mass of zinc, in tonnes, that is produced from 20 tonnes of zinc oxide.

**b**   Nitrogen and hydrogen react together to form ammonia.

$$N_2 + 3H_2 \rightarrow 2NH_3$$

When the reaction is complete, 14 tonnes of nitrogen are converted into 17 tonnes of ammonia. How much nitrogen will be needed to produce 34 tonnes of ammonia?

**c**   The sugar lactose, $C_{12}H_{22}O_{11}$, is sometimes used in place of charcoal in fireworks.

State the total number of atoms present in a molecule of lactose. ....................................

**d**   A molecule of compound **Y** contains the following atoms bonded covalently together:
   - 2 atoms of carbon (C)
   - 2 atoms of oxygen (O)
   - 4 atoms of hydrogen (H).

What is the formula of a molecule of **Y**? ....................................

# Exercise 6.3 Calculating the percentage of certain elements in a compound and empirical formulae

> This exercise will develop your skills in processing calculations on formula mass and empirical formulae.

**a** Complete the diagram to work out the formula mass of the iron oxide in the ore magnetite. (Relative atomic masses: Fe = 56, O = 16.) Then use the steps below to work out the percentage by mass of iron in this ore.

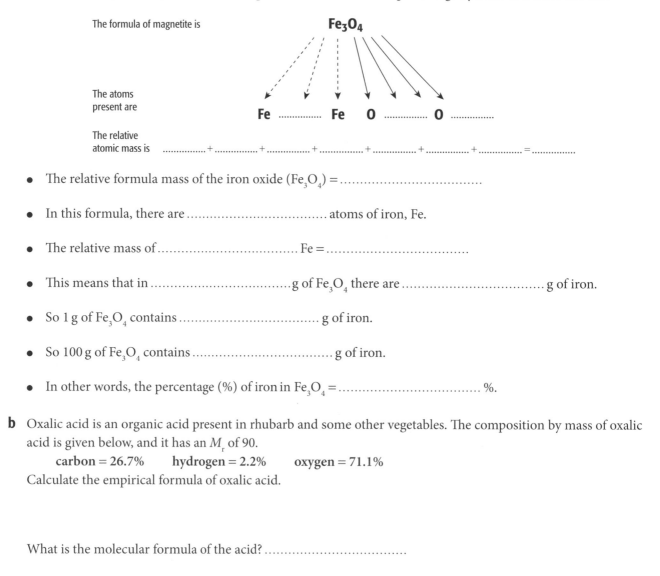

The formula of magnetite is $Fe_3O_4$

The atoms present are

Fe ............... Fe    O ............... O ...............

The relative atomic mass is    ............... + ............... + ............... + ............... + ............... + ............... + ............... = ...............

- The relative formula mass of the iron oxide ($Fe_3O_4$) = ...................................

- In this formula, there are ................................... atoms of iron, Fe.

- The relative mass of ................................... Fe = ...................................

- This means that in ................................... g of $Fe_3O_4$ there are ................................... g of iron.

- So 1 g of $Fe_3O_4$ contains ................................... g of iron.

- So 100 g of $Fe_3O_4$ contains ................................... g of iron.

- In other words, the percentage (%) of iron in $Fe_3O_4$ = ................................... %.

**b** Oxalic acid is an organic acid present in rhubarb and some other vegetables. The composition by mass of oxalic acid is given below, and it has an $M_r$ of 90.

carbon = 26.7%    hydrogen = 2.2%    oxygen = 71.1%

Calculate the empirical formula of oxalic acid.



What is the molecular formula of the acid? ...................................

**c** A volatile arsenic compound containing arsenic, carbon and hydrogen has the following composition by mass:

arsenic = 62.5%    carbon = 30.0%    hydrogen = 7.5%

Calculate the empirical formula of this compound.

# Exercise 6.4   Calculations involving solutions

> This exercise will help develop your understanding of the idea of the mole and its application to the concentration of solutions. It will develop your skills in processing practical data from titrations.

## Testing the purity of citric acid

Citric acid is an organic acid which is a white solid at room temperature. It dissolves readily in water.

The purity of a sample of the acid was tested by the following method.

- Step 1: A sample of 0.48 g citric acid was dissolved in 50 cm³ of distilled water.
- Step 2: Drops of phenolphthalein indicator were added (see page 141 in the Coursebook for the colour change of this indicator).
- Step 3: The solution was then titrated with a solution of sodium hydroxide (0.50 mol/dm³).

**a  i**   Complete the labels for the pieces of apparatus used and give the colour of the solution before titration.

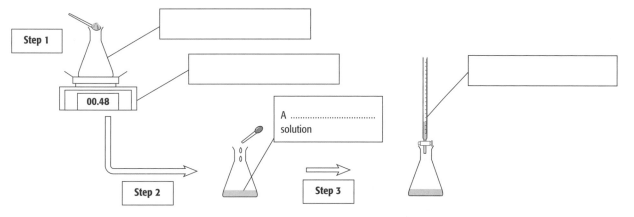

**ii**   These were the burette readings from the titration. Complete the table by filling in the missing value (*P*).

| Final burette reading / cm³ | 14.60 |
|---|---|
| First burette reading / cm³ | 0.20 |
| Volume of NaOH(aq) added / cm³ | ............................ (*P*) |

**b**   Calculate the purity of the citric acid by following the stages outlined here.
1st stage: Calculate the number of moles of alkali solution reacted in the titration.

- *P* cm³ of NaOH(aq) containing 0.50 moles in 1000 cm³ were used.

- Number of moles NaOH used $= \dfrac{0.50}{1000} \times P = Q =$ .................................... moles.

2nd stage: Calculate the number of moles of citric acid in the sample.

- Note that one mole of citric acid reacts with three moles of sodium hydroxide.

- Then number of moles of citric acid in sample $= \dfrac{Q}{3} = R =$ .................................... moles.

**3rd stage:** Calculate the mass of citric acid in the sample and therefore the percentage purity.

- Relative formula mass of citric acid ($M_r$ of $C_6H_8O_7$) =.....................................
  ($C = 12$, $H = 1$, $O = 16$)

- Mass of citric acid in sample = $R \times M_r = S =$..................................... g.

- Percentage purity of sample = $\dfrac{S}{0.48}$ =.....................................%.

**c** How could the sample of citric acid be purified further?

.................................................................................................................................................

.................................................................................................................................................

## Finding the percentage yield of hydrated copper(II) sulfate

Hydrated crystals of copper(II) sulfate-5-water were prepared by the following reactions:

$$CuO(s) + H_2SO_4(aq) \rightarrow CuSO_4(aq) + H_2O(l)$$
$$CuSO_4(aq) + 5H_2O(l) \rightarrow CuSO_4 \cdot 5H_2O(s)$$

In an experiment, 25.00 cm³ of 2.0 mol/dm³ sulfuric acid was neutralised with an excess of copper(II) oxide. The yield of crystals, $CuSO_4 \cdot 5H_2O$, was 7.3 g.

**d** Complete the following to calculate the percentage yield.

- Number of moles of $H_2SO_4$ in 25.00 cm³ of 2.0 mol/dm³ solution =.....................................

- Maximum number of moles of $CuSO_4 \cdot 5H_2O$ that could be formed =.....................................

- Maximum mass of crystals, $CuSO_4 \cdot 5H_2O$, that could be formed =.....................................
  (The mass of one mole of $CuSO_4 \cdot 5H_2O$ is 250 g.)

- Percentage yield =..................................... %

# Exercise 6.5 Finding the mass of 5 cm of magnesium ribbon

> This exercise will develop your skills in handling experimental data in novel situations.

From the chemical equation for the reaction and using the relative formula masses together with the molar volume of a gas it is possible to predict the amounts of magnesium sulfate and hydrogen that are produced when 24 g of magnesium are reacted with excess sulfuric acid.

This relationship between the mass of magnesium used and the volume of gas produced can be used to find the mass of a short piece of magnesium ribbon indirectly.

## Apparatus and method

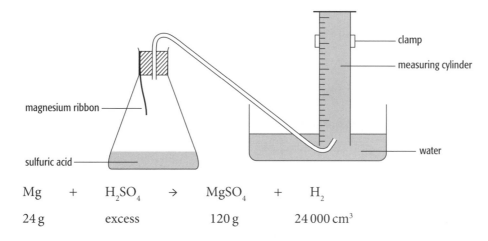

$$Mg \quad + \quad H_2SO_4 \quad \rightarrow \quad MgSO_4 \quad + \quad H_2$$

24 g       excess       120 g       24 000 cm³

The experimental instructions were as follows.

- **Wear safety goggles for eye protection.**
- Set up the apparatus as shown in the diagram with 25 cm³ of sulfuric acid in the flask.
- Make sure the measuring cylinder is completely full of water.
- Carefully measure 5 cm of magnesium ribbon and grip it below the flask stopper as shown.
- Ease the stopper up to release the ribbon and immediately replace it.
- When no further bubbles rise into the measuring cylinder, record the volume of gas collected.
- Repeat the experiment twice more using 5 cm of magnesium ribbon and fresh sulfuric acid each time.
- Find the average volume of hydrogen produced.

## Data handling

A student obtained the results shown in the table when measuring the volume of hydrogen produced.

| Experiment number | Volume of hydrogen collected / cm³ |
|---|---|
| 1 | 85 |
| 2 | 79 |
| 3 | 82 |
| average | .............. |

**a** Fill in the average of the results obtained. Can you think of possible reasons why the three results are not the same?

...................................................................................................................................................

**b** You know that 24 g of magnesium will produce 24 000 cm³ of hydrogen. What mass of magnesium would be needed to produce your volume of hydrogen?

...................................................................................................................................................

...................................................................................................................................................

This is the mass of 5 cm of magnesium ribbon. The weight is too low to weigh easily on a balance but you could weigh a longer length and use that to check your answer.

**c** What mass of magnesium sulfate would you expect 5 cm of magnesium ribbon to produce?

...................................................................................................................................................

...................................................................................................................................................

**d** Plan an experiment to check whether your prediction above is correct.

...................................................................................................................................................

...................................................................................................................................................

## Ⓢ Exercise 6.6  Reacting volumes of gases

> There is a direct relationship between the volume of a gas and the number of moles present in the sample.
> This exercise gives you an example of how to use that relationship for a particular experiment.

Experiments show that volumes of gases react together in a ratio that can be predicted from the chemical equation for the reaction.

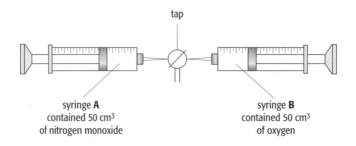

tap

syringe **A**
contained 50 cm³
of nitrogen monoxide

syringe **B**
contained 50 cm³
of oxygen

Under the conditions used here, nitrogen monoxide (NO) reacts with oxygen (O₂) to form one product that is a brown gas. In an experiment, 5.0 cm³ portions of oxygen were pushed from syringe **B** into syringe **A**.

**s** After each addition, the tap was closed, the gases were cooled, and then the total volume of gases remaining was measured. The results are shown in the graph.

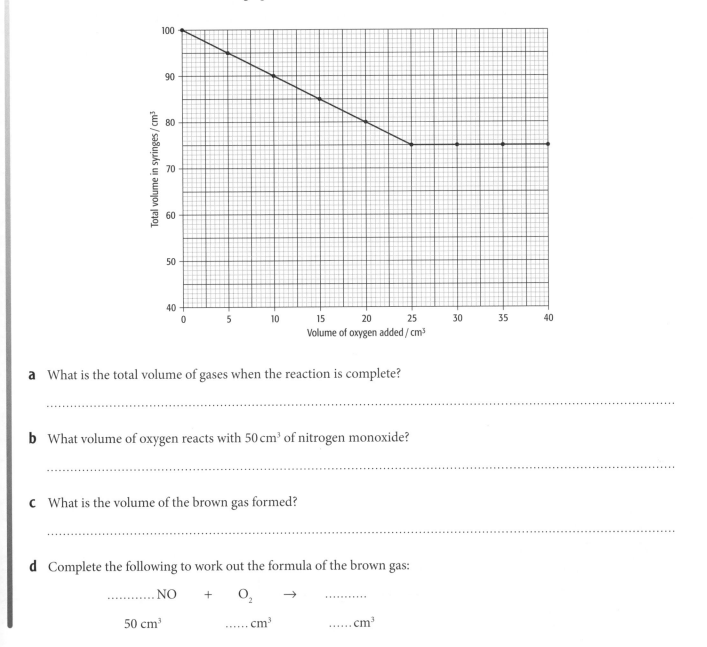

**a** What is the total volume of gases when the reaction is complete?

...................................................................................................................................................................................

**b** What volume of oxygen reacts with 50 cm³ of nitrogen monoxide?

...................................................................................................................................................................................

**c** What is the volume of the brown gas formed?

...................................................................................................................................................................................

**d** Complete the following to work out the formula of the brown gas:

.............NO      +      $O_2$      →      ...........

    50 cm³               ...... cm³          ...... cm³

# Exercise 6.7 Calculation triangles

The conversion of the mass of a sample into moles and vice versa is central to chemical calculations because it gives us a measure of the number of atoms and/or molecules involved in reactions. This exercise will help you become familiar with the use of the calculation 'triangles' that are a memory aid to these conversions.

## a Converting masses to moles, and moles to masses

Fill in the calculation triangle for changing between masses and moles. Then complete the table below. (Use the following $A_r$ values: H = 1, C = 12, N = 14, O = 16, Mg = 24, S = 32, Cl = 35.5, Ca = 40, Cu = 64.)

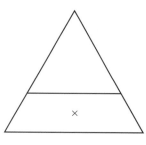

| Substance | $A_r$ or $M_r$ | Number of moles | Mass / g |
|---|---|---|---|
| Cu | | | 128 |
| Mg | | 0.5 | |
| $Cl_2$ | | | 35.5 |
| $H_2$ | | | 4 |
| $S_8$ | | 2 | |
| $O_3$ | | | 1.6 |
| $H_2SO_4$ | | 2.5 | |
| $CO_2$ | | 0.4 | |
| $NH_3$ | | | 25.5 |
| $CaCO_3$ | | | 100 |
| $MgSO_4 \cdot 7H_2O$ | | | 82 |

**ⓢ b   Calculations involving solutions**

Fill in the calculation triangle relating moles of solute to volume and concentration. Then complete the table below.

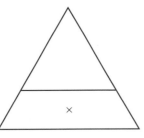

| Solute | Volume of solution | Concentration of solution / mol/dm³ | Moles of solute present |
|---|---|---|---|
| sodium chloride | 1 dm³ | 0.5 | |
| hydrochloric acid | 500 cm³ | 0.5 | |
| sodium hydroxide | 2 dm³ | | 1 |
| sulfuric acid | 250 cm³ | | 0.5 |
| sodium thiosulfate | | 2 | 0.4 |
| copper(II) sulfate | | 0.1 | 0.75 |

# Exercise 6.8   Scaling up!

> One aspect of carrying out calculations in chemistry is the scaling up of the amounts used to industrial proportions. This exercise gives you some practice at that and at calculating the percentage yield of reactions.

In the laboratory, we are used to working with grams of material and our calculations are usually framed on that basis. However, an industrial chemist is often used to working on a significantly larger scale and looking to produce tonnes of product.

**a**   In this context, it is useful to know that the reacting proportions determined by the equation for the reaction can be readily scaled up to provide useful data at an industrial level.

**i**   What mass of iron(III) oxide is needed to produce 100 g of iron, in the blast furnace? Complete the sentence below using your calculated figures. (Use the following $A_r$ values: C = 12; O = 16; Fe = 56.)

The equation for the reaction is:
$Fe_2O_3(s) + 3CO(g) \rightarrow 2Fe(s) + 3CO_2(g)$

..................................................................................................................................................................

..................................................................................................................................................................

..................................................................................................................................................................

100 g of iron is ...................... moles of Fe, so ............... moles of $Fe_2O_3$ are needed for the reaction,

or .................... g of iron(III) oxide.

**ii** Using your calculated value for how much iron(III) oxide (hematite) is needed to produce 100 g of iron, state how much hematite is needed to produce 50 tonnes of iron.

.................................................................................................................................................

.................................................................................................................................................

**iii** Realistically, industrial processes and laboratory experiments do not produce perfect yields. In a particular blast furnace run, 100 tonnes of hematite gave 7 tonnes of iron. Calculate the percentage yield of the process.

.................................................................................................................................................

.................................................................................................................................................

.................................................................................................................................................

.................................................................................................................................................

**b** Another large-scale industrial process is the production of quicklime from limestone by heating in a lime kiln.

**i** What is the equation for the thermal decomposition of limestone?

.................................................................................................................................................

**ii** Using your equation, calculate how many tonnes of quicklime would be produced from 1 tonne of limestone. ($A_r$ of Ca = 40)

.................................................................................................................................................

.................................................................................................................................................

.................................................................................................................................................

**iii** In one production run, 2.5 tonnes of limestone were found to give 1.12 tonnes of quicklime. What is the percentage yield for this process? Give **one** reason why this yield is not 100%.

.................................................................................................................................................

.................................................................................................................................................

.................................................................................................................................................

.................................................................................................................................................

# 7 How far? How fast?

# Exercise 7.1 Terms of reaction

This exercise should help you familiarise yourself with certain key terms relating to the progress of chemical reactions.

Draw lines to match the terms on the left with the correct statement on the right.

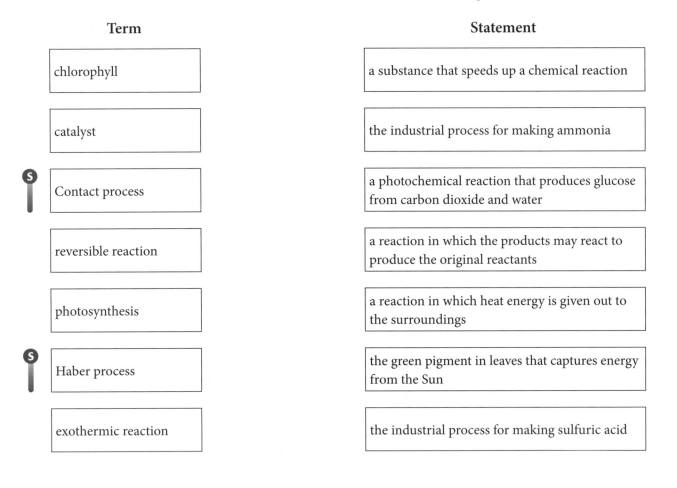

Term

chlorophyll

catalyst

Contact process

reversible reaction

photosynthesis

Haber process

exothermic reaction

Statement

a substance that speeds up a chemical reaction

the industrial process for making ammonia

a photochemical reaction that produces glucose from carbon dioxide and water

a reaction in which the products may react to produce the original reactants

a reaction in which heat energy is given out to the surroundings

the green pigment in leaves that captures energy from the Sun

the industrial process for making sulfuric acid

# Exercise 7.2   Energy diagrams

This exercise is aimed at helping you understand energy level diagrams and their usefulness in showing why some reactions are exothermic while others are endothermic.

**a** The energy changes involved in chemical reactions can be represented visually by energy level diagrams. Such diagrams show the relative stability of the reactants and products. The more stable a set of reactants or products, the lower their energy level.

The energy level diagram for an exothermic reaction is different from that for an endothermic reaction. The following keywords/phrases will be needed to fill in the information boxes accompanying the diagrams.

**given out       positive       taken in       reactants       negative       products**

**i**   Exothermic reactions

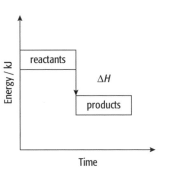

Use information from the diagram and the keywords/phrases to complete the following information box.

In an exothermic reaction, the ...................................... have more energy than

the ............................................. .

This means that ΔH is ............................................. .

The difference in energy is ............................................. as heat.

The temperature of the surroundings **increases/decreases**. (*Delete the incorrect word.*)

**ii**   Endothermic reactions

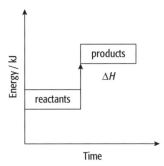

Again, use information from the diagram and the keywords/phrases to complete the following information box.

In an endothermic reaction, the ....................................... have more energy

than the .................................................. .

This means that $\Delta H$ is ................................................ .

The difference in energy is ................................................ from the surroundings.

The temperature of the surroundings **increases/decreases**. (*Delete the incorrect word.*)

**S** **b** The following is a table of bond energies.

| Bond | Bond energy/kJ per mole |
|------|-------------------------|
| C—C | 347 |
| C—H | 413 |
| C=O | 805 |
| O=O | 498 |
| O—H | 464 |

**i** Use the values given to calculate the heat of combustion of propane.

The equation for the combustion of propane is:

$$C_3H_8(g) + 5O_2(g) \rightarrow 3CO_2(g) + 4H_2O(g)$$

.................................................................................................................................................

.................................................................................................................................................

.................................................................................................................................................

.................................................................................................................................................

.................................................................................................................................................

.................................................................................................................................................

**ii** Draw an energy level diagram for this reaction.




**iii** How much energy is released when the following amounts of propane are burnt?

($A_r$ values: C = 12; H = 1.)

0.2 mol: ...........................

.................................................................................................................................................................

.................................................................................................................................................................

4 mol: ...........................

.................................................................................................................................................................

.................................................................................................................................................................

33 g: ...........................

.................................................................................................................................................................

.................................................................................................................................................................

## Ⓢ Exercise 7.3   The collision theory of reaction rates

> **This exercise should help you develop an understanding of the collision (particle) theory of reactions and how changing conditions affect the rate of various types of reaction.**

Complete the following table from your understanding of the factors that affect the speed (rate) of a reaction. Several of the sections have been completed already. The finished table should then be a useful revision aid.

| Factor affecting the reaction | Types of reaction affected | Change made in the condition | Effect on rate of reaction |
|---|---|---|---|
| concentration | all reactions involving solutions or reactions involving gases | an increase in the concentration of one, or both, of the ........................ means there are more particles in the same volume | increases the rate of reaction as the particles ........................ more frequently |
| pressure | reactions involving ........................ only | an increase in the pressure | greatly ........................ the rate of reaction – the effect is the same as that of an increase in ........................ |
| temperature | all reactions | an increase in temperature – this means that molecules are moving ........................ and collide more ........................; the particles also have more ........................ when they collide | ........................ the rate of reaction |
| particle size | reactions involving solids and liquids, solids and gases or mixtures of solids | use the same mass of a solid but make the pieces of solid ........................ | greatly increases the rate of reaction |

*(Continued)*

| Factor affecting the reaction | Types of reaction affected | Change made in the condition | Effect on rate of reaction |
|---|---|---|---|
| light | a number of photochemical reactions including photosynthesis, the reaction between methane and chlorine, and the reaction on photographic film | reaction in the presence of<br><br>......................<br><br>or UV light | greatly increases the rate of reaction |
| using a catalyst | slow reactions can be speeded up by adding a suitable catalyst | reduces amount of<br><br>......................<br><br>required for the reaction to take place:<br>the catalyst is present in the same<br><br>......................<br><br>at the end of the reaction | ......................<br><br>the rate of reaction |

# Exercise 7.4    The influence of surface area on the rate of reaction

> This exercise should help develop your skills in presenting and manipulating experimental data. You will also be asked to interpret data and draw conclusions from it.

A useful experiment that shows the effect of varying the surface area of a solid on reaction rate is based on the fact that hydrochloric acid reacts with calcium carbonate to produce the gas carbon dioxide.

The experiment was set up as shown below using identical masses of marble chips. Flask **A** contains larger pieces of marble chips and Flask **B** contains smaller pieces. The same concentration and volume of acid was used in both flasks.

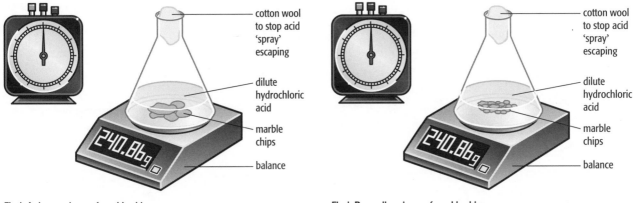

cotton wool to stop acid 'spray' escaping

dilute hydrochloric acid

marble chips

balance

Flask A: larger pieces of marble chips

cotton wool to stop acid 'spray' escaping

dilute hydrochloric acid

marble chips

balance

Flask B: smaller pieces of marble chips

The flasks were quickly and simultaneously set to zero on the balances. The mass loss of the flasks was then recorded over time.

**a** Write the word equation for the reaction between marble chips (calcium carbonate) and dilute hydrochloric acid.

..............................................................................................................................................................................

**b** What causes the loss in mass from the flasks?

..............................................................................................................................................................................

..............................................................................................................................................................................

Readings on the digital balance were taken every 30 seconds. The balance had been tared to zero at the start of the reaction.
For the large pieces of marble chips (Flask **A**), readings (in g) were:

  0.00   −0.21   −0.46   −0.65   −0.76   −0.81   −0.91

−0.92   −0.96   −0.98   −0.98   −1.00   −0.99   −0.99

For the small pieces of marble chips (Flask **B**), readings (in g) were:

  0.00   −0.51   −0.78   −0.87   −0.91   −0.94   −0.96

−0.98   −0.99   −0.99   −0.99   −1.00   −0.99   −1.00

**c** Create a suitable table showing how the mass of carbon dioxide produced (equal to the loss of mass) varies with time for the two experiments.

**d** Plot the **two** graphs on the grid.

**e** Which pieces gave the faster rate of reaction? Explain why.

..................................................................................................................................

..................................................................................................................................

..................................................................................................................................

**f** Explain why, for both flasks, the same amount of gas is produced in the end.

..................................................................................................................................

..................................................................................................................................

..................................................................................................................................

Use the checklist below to give yourself a mark for your graph.
For each point, award yourself:
2 marks if you did it really well
1 mark if you made a good attempt at it, and partly succeeded
0 marks if you did not try to do it, or did not succeed.

**Self-assessment checklist for graphs:**

| Check point | Marks awarded | |
| --- | --- | --- |
| | You | Your teacher |
| You have drawn the axes with a ruler, using most of the width and height of the grid. | | |
| You have used a good scale for the $x$-axis and the $y$-axis, going up in 0.25s, 0.5s, 1s or 2s. | | |
| You have labelled the axes correctly, giving the correct units for the scales on both axes. | | |
| You have plotted each point precisely and correctly. | | |
| You have used a small, neat cross or dot for each point. | | |
| You have drawn a single, clear best-fit line through each set of points. | | |
| You have ignored any anomalous results when drawing the line through each set of points. | | |
| Total (out of 14) | | |

| 12–14 | Excellent. |
| --- | --- |
| 10–11 | Good. |
| 7–9 | A good start, but you need to improve quite a bit. |
| 5–6 | Poor. Try this same graph again, using a new sheet of graph paper. |
| 1–4 | Very poor. Read through all the criteria again, and then try the same graph again. |

# Exercise 7.5 Finding the rate of a reaction producing a gas

This exercise is based on an important practical technique of gas collection using a gas syringe. Following through the exercise should help develop your skills in presenting experimental data and calculating results from it. You will also be asked how the experiment could be modified to provide further data.

Hydrogen peroxide, $H_2O_2$, is an unstable compound that decomposes slowly at room temperature to form water and oxygen.

$$2H_2O_2(aq) \rightarrow 2H_2O(l) + O_2(g)$$

A student investigated how the rate of decomposition depends on the catalyst. She tested two catalysts: manganese(IV) oxide (experiment **1**) and copper (experiment **2**). The volume of oxygen produced by the reaction was measured at different times using the apparatus shown.

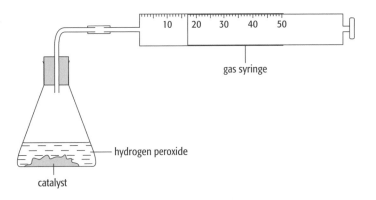

gas syringe

hydrogen peroxide

catalyst

**a** Use the data from the diagrams below to complete the results for experiment **2** in the following table.

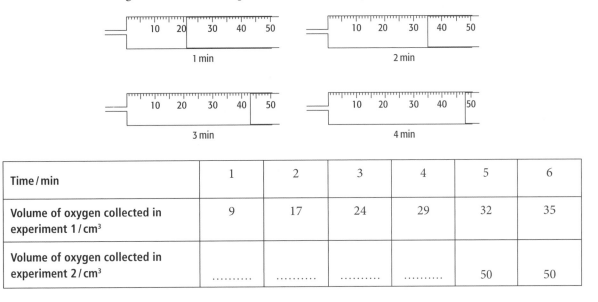

1 min

2 min

3 min

4 min

| Time / min | 1 | 2 | 3 | 4 | 5 | 6 |
|---|---|---|---|---|---|---|
| Volume of oxygen collected in experiment 1 / cm³ | 9 | 17 | 24 | 29 | 32 | 35 |
| Volume of oxygen collected in experiment 2 / cm³ | .......... | .......... | .......... | .......... | 50 | 50 |

**b** Plot the results from experiments **1** and **2** on the grid and draw a smooth curve through each set of points. Label the curves you draw as **exp.1** and **exp.2**.

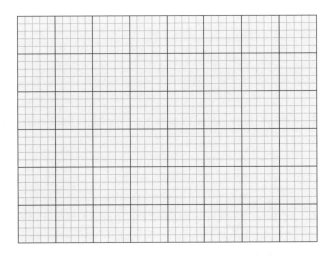

**c** Which of the two experiments was the first to reach completion? Explain your answer.

.................................................................................................................................................

.................................................................................................................................................

.................................................................................................................................................

**d** Use your graph to estimate the time taken in experiment **1** to double the volume of oxygen produced from $15\,cm^3$ to $30\,cm^3$. Record your answers in the table, and indicate on the graph how you obtained your values.

| Time taken to produce $30\,cm^3$/min | .................... |
|---|---|
| Time taken to produce $15\,cm^3$/min | .................... |
| Time taken to double the volume from $15\,cm^3$ to $30\,cm^3$/min | .................... |

Experiment 1 (using manganese(IV) oxide)

**e** The rate (or speed) of a reaction may be calculated using the formula:

$$\text{rate of reaction} = \frac{\text{volume of oxygen produced}/cm^3}{\text{time taken}/min}$$

Using the two graphs and the above formula, calculate the rate of each reaction after the first 2.5 min for each experiment.

**f** From your answer to **e**, suggest which is the better catalyst, manganese(IV) oxide or copper. Explain your answer.

.................................................................................................................................................

.................................................................................................................................................

**g** At the end of experiment 2 the copper was removed from the solution by filtration. It was dried and weighed. How would you predict this mass of copper would compare with the mass of copper added at the start of the experiment? Explain your answer.

.................................................................................................................................................

.................................................................................................................................................

**h** Suggest how the rate of decomposition in either experiment could be further increased.

.................................................................................................................................

.................................................................................................................................

.................................................................................................................................

# Exercise 7.6 Runaway reactions

This exercise is designed to introduce the idea of 'runaway reactions' and to develop your data handling and interpretation skills.

A runaway reaction is a reaction which becomes uncontrollable. A common example is a reaction which is highly exothermic. During an exothermic reaction, the reaction mixture increases in temperature, and this further increases the rate of reaction. Heat is then produced more rapidly and the rate increases further. In an industrial process, this can cause an explosion and great danger to people living around the site.

A student carried out an investigation using the reaction between magnesium and sulfuric acid. He was investigating ways of controlling very exothermic reactions.

In each experiment, he took $10\,cm^3$ of sulfuric acid, noted its temperature and then added $0.1\,g$ of magnesium ribbon. He measured the volume of gas produced in the first 30 seconds of the reaction and noted the temperature when the reaction stopped.

To make the reaction a fair test, he kept the amounts of magnesium and sulfuric acid the same in each experiment, but he changed the conditions by adding a different volume of water to the acid in each case before adding the magnesium.

The student's results are shown in the table opposite.

| Volume of water added / $cm^3$ | Concentration of acid / $mol/dm^3$ | Starting temperature / °C | Final temperature / °C | Temperature change / °C | Volume of gas collected in 30 seconds / $cm^3$ |
|---|---|---|---|---|---|
| 0 | 1.0 | 21 | 53 | 32 | 42 |
| 5 | | 21 | 44 | | 27 |
| 10 | | 21 | 38 | | 21 |
| 15 | | 21 | 34 | | 17 |
| 20 | | 21 | 30 | | 13 |
| 30 | | 21 | 27 | | 10 |
| 40 | 0.20 | 21 | 25 | 4 | 7 |

**a** Complete the table by filling in the second and fifth columns.

**b** Plot graphs of the data on the grid provided.

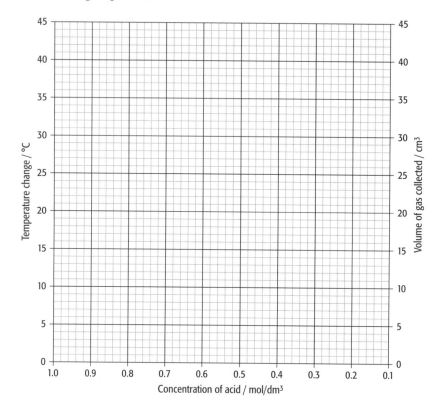

**c** Unusually, the horizontal ($x$) axis has been shown with a **decreasing** scale of concentration values.

**i** If concentration is decreasing, what property of the solution is increasing?

.................................................................................................................................................................

**ii** What effect is plotting the graphs in this way designed to emphasise?

.................................................................................................................................................................

.................................................................................................................................................................

**d** Why can you be sure that the amount of energy produced in each reaction is the same?

.................................................................................................................................................................

**e** Why is the temperature change different in each case?

.................................................................................................................................................................

**f** What do the volumes of gas collected tell you about the rate of the different reactions?

.................................................................................................................................................................

.................................................................................................................................................................

**g** In industry, three things are important:

- safety (of the factory, the workers and the environment)
- how much product is made (the more the better)
- how quickly the product is produced (the more quickly the better).

Bearing this in mind, what advice would you give a factory that was going to use the reaction between magnesium and sulfuric acid on a large scale?

..............................................................................................................................................................

..............................................................................................................................................................

..............................................................................................................................................................

..............................................................................................................................................................

..............................................................................................................................................................

Use the checklist below to give yourself a mark for your graph.
For each point, award yourself:
2 marks if you did it really well
1 mark if you made a good attempt at it, and partly succeeded
0 marks if you did not try to do it, or did not succeed.

**Self-assessment checklist for graphs:**

| Check point | Marks awarded | |
| --- | --- | --- |
| | You | Your teacher |
| You have plotted each point precisely and correctly for both sets of data – using the different scales on the two horizontal axes. | | |
| You have used a small, neat cross or dot for the points of one graph. | | |
| You have used a small, but different, symbol for the points of the other graph. | | |
| You have drawn a best-fit line through one set of points. | | |
| You have drawn a best-fit line through the other set of points using a different colour or broken line. | | |
| You have ignored any anomalous results when drawing the lines. | | |
| **Total (out of 12)** | | |

10–12    Excellent.
7–9      Good.
4–6      A good start, but you need to improve quite a bit.
2–3      Poor. Try this same graph again, using a new sheet of graph paper.
1        Very poor. Read through all the criteria again, and then try the same graph again.

# Exercise 7.7 CCS (carbon capture and storage)

> The levels of carbon dioxide and other greenhouse gases in the atmosphere are a continuing cause of concern. This exercise discusses some of the chemistry of a method of carbon capture and other aspects of the threat of global warming.

Power stations, vehicles using petrol and diesel fuels, and many industries produce carbon dioxide which is released into the air. Carbon dioxide is a 'greenhouse gas'. Because carbon dioxide builds up in the atmosphere faster than it can be removed by the photosynthesis of plants, there is a danger of global warming.

There are ways of removing the carbon dioxide from gases produced by industry (carbon capture) and this carbon dioxide could then be stored (underground).

The equation shows one reaction which can be used to 'capture' carbon dioxide.

$$K_2CO_3(aq) + H_2O(l) + CO_2(g) \rightleftharpoons 2KHCO_3(aq)$$

This reaction is exothermic.

**a** What is global warming and why is it a problem?

......................................................................................................................................

......................................................................................................................................

......................................................................................................................................

**b** Carbon dioxide is a greenhouse gas. Give an example of another greenhouse gas and state one of its sources.

......................................................................................................................................

......................................................................................................................................

**c** How can you tell from the equation that the reaction above is reversible?

......................................................................................................................................

**d** Suggest how the reaction could be reversed to reclaim the carbon dioxide.

......................................................................................................................................

**e** Why is this a good/economical reaction to use to remove carbon dioxide produced in exhaust gases?

......................................................................................................................................

......................................................................................................................................

**f** Scientists have recently drawn attention to a new source of methane for the atmosphere. They have identified thousands of sites in the Arctic where methane that has been stored for many millennia is now bubbling into the atmosphere. The methane has been trapped by ice but it is able to escape as the ice melts.

Methane is the second most important greenhouse gas and this release as the ice and permafrost melt is predicted to have significant environmental consequences.

The methane molecules are trapped within 'cages' of water molecules in what is sometimes referred to as 'methane ice'.

**i** What is the structural formula of methane?

**ii** Write the word and symbol equations for the complete combustion of methane in air.

......................................................................................................................................

......................................................................................................................................

## Exercise 7.8   Reversible reactions involving inter-halogen compounds

> The aim of this exercise is to develop your ability to apply your knowledge to experimental situations that you will not previously have met.

The following experiment was carried out in a fume cupboard. A few crystals of iodine were placed at the bottom of a U-tube and chlorine gas was passed over them. The tube became warm and a brown liquid, iodine monochloride (ICl), was formed.

**a**   Why was the experiment carried out in a fume cupboard?

.......................................................................................................................................................................

.......................................................................................................................................................................

**b**   What evidence is there that a chemical reaction took place between the iodine and the chlorine?

.......................................................................................................................................................................

.......................................................................................................................................................................

**c**   Write the balanced equation for the formation of iodine monochloride.

.......................................................................................................................................................................

The experiment was continued further, as shown in the following sequence of diagrams.

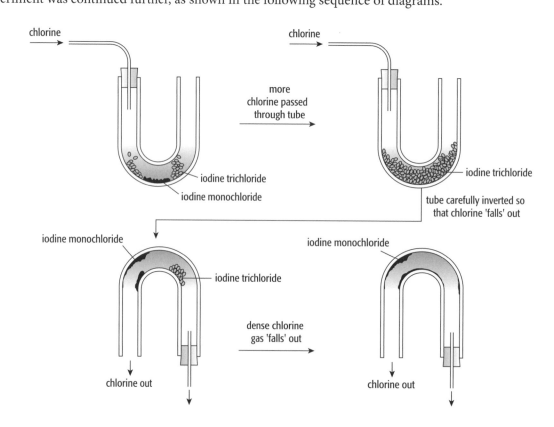

**s** **d** What conclusions can be drawn from this experiment?

..................................................................................................................................................

..................................................................................................................................................

..................................................................................................................................................

**e** Write balanced equations for any reactions that occur following the initial formation of iodine monochloride.

..................................................................................................................................................

..................................................................................................................................................

..................................................................................................................................................

# 8 Patterns and properties of metals

## Definitions to learn

- **alkali metal** a reactive metal in Group I of the Periodic Table; alkali metals react with water to produce alkaline solutions
- **transition metal** a metal in the central block of the Periodic Table; transition metals are hard, dense metals that form coloured compounds and can have more than one valency
- **reactivity series** a listing of the metals in order of their reactivity
- **electrochemical cell** a cell made up of two metal electrodes of different reactivity placed in an electrolyte; the voltage set up depends on the difference in reactivity between the two metals

## Useful equations

$2Na + 2H_2O \rightarrow 2NaOH + H_2$

$Fe_2O_3 + 2Al \rightarrow Al_2O_3 + 2Fe$

$Zn(s) + CuSO_4(aq) \rightarrow ZnSO_4(aq) + Cu(s)$

$2KNO_3(s) \rightarrow 2KNO_2(s) + O_2(g)$

$2Pb(NO_3)_2(s) \rightarrow 2PbO(s) + 4NO_2(g) + O_2(g)$

## Exercise 8.1  Group I: The alkali metals

This exercise should help you learn certain key properties of the alkali metals, and help develop the skills of predicting the properties of unfamiliar elements from the features of those that you have learnt.

Caesium is an alkali metal. It is in Group I of the Periodic Table.

**a** State **two** physical properties of caesium.

.................................................................................................................................

.................................................................................................................................

**b** State the number of electrons in the outer shell of a caesium atom. ...........................................

**c** Complete the table below to estimate the boiling point and atomic radius of caesium. Comment also on the reactivity of potassium and caesium with water.

| Group I metal | Density/g/cm³ | Radius of metal atom/nm | Boiling point/°C | Reactivity with water |
|---|---|---|---|---|
| sodium | 0.97 | 0.191 | 883 | floats and fizzes quickly on the surface, disappears gradually and does not burst into flame |
| potassium | 0.86 | 0.235 | 760 | ...................................... ...................................... ...................................... |
| rubidium | 1.53 | 0.250 | 686 | reacts instantaneously, fizzes and bursts into flame then spits violently and may explode |
| caesium | 1.88 | ...................... | ...................... | ...................................... ...................................... ...................................... |

**d** Write the word equation for the reaction of caesium with water.

......................................................................................................................................

# Exercise 8.2  The reactivity series of metals

This exercise should help you familiarise yourself with certain aspects of the reactivity series. It should also help develop your skills in interpreting practical observations and predicting the properties of unfamiliar elements from the features of those that you have learnt.

Using the results of various different types of chemical reaction, the metals can be arranged into the reactivity series.

**a** Magnesium reacts very slowly indeed with cold water but it does react strongly with steam to give magnesium oxide and a gas. Write the word equation for the reaction between magnesium and steam.

......................................................................................................................................

**b** Choose **one** metal from the reactivity series that will not react with steam.

.................................................................................................................................................................................

**c** Choose **one** metal from the reactivity series that will safely react with dilute sulfuric acid.

.................................................................................................................................................................................

**d** In each of the experiments below, a piece of metal is placed in a solution of a metal salt. Complete the table of observations.

| | | zinc | zinc | tin | silver | copper |
|---|---|---|---|---|---|---|
| | | tin(II) chloride solution | copper(II) sulfate solution | copper(II) sulfate solution | copper(II) sulfate solution | silver nitrate solution |
| **At start** | colour of metal | grey | ..................... | silver-coloured | silver-coloured | ..................... |
| | colour of solution | colourless | ..................... | blue | blue | colourless |
| **At finish** | colour of metal | coated with silver-coloured crystals | ..................... | coated with brown solid | silver-coloured | coated with silver-coloured crystals |
| | colour of solution | colourless | ..................... | colourless | blue | ..................... |

**e** Use these results to place the metals **copper**, **silver**, **tin** and **zinc** in order of reactivity (putting the most reactive metal first).

................................................ > ................................................ > ................................................ > ................................................

The reactivity series of metals given in the box contains both familiar and unfamiliar elements. The unfamiliar elements are marked with an asterisk (*) and their common oxidation states are given. Choose metal(s) from this list to answer the following questions.

| barium* | Ba (+2) |
| lanthanum* | La (+3) |
| aluminium | |
| zinc | |
| chromium* | Cr (+2),(+3),(+6) |
| iron | |
| copper | |
| palladium* | Pd (+2) |

**f** Which **two** metals would not react with dilute hydrochloric acid?

......................................................................................................................................................

**g** Which **two** unfamiliar metals would react with cold water?

......................................................................................................................................................

**h** Name an unfamiliar metal that could not be extracted from its oxide by reduction with carbon.

......................................................................................................................................................

**i** Why should you be able to predict that metals such as iron and chromium have more than one oxidation state?

......................................................................................................................................................

# Exercise 8.3   Energy from displacement reactions

This exercise will help you practise the presentation and interpretation of practical experiments.

When a metal is added to a solution of the salt of a less reactive metal, a displacement reaction takes place. The equations for two different examples are:

$$Fe(s) + CuSO_4(aq) \rightarrow Cu(s) + FeSO_4(aq)$$
zinc + copper sulfate → copper + zinc sulfate

The energy change involved in these reactions can be measured by adding 5 g of metal powder to 50 cm$^3$ of 0.5 mol/dm$^3$ copper (II) sulfate solution in a polystyrene cup. The temperature of the solution is taken before adding the metal. The powder is then added, the reaction mixture is stirred continuously, and temperatures are taken every 30 seconds for 3 minutes.

A student took the readings that follow when carrying out this experiment.

| Time / min | 0.0 | 0.5 | 1.0 | 1.5 | 2.0 | 2.5 | 3.0 |
|---|---|---|---|---|---|---|---|
| Experiment 1 (zinc): temperature / °C | 21 | 48 | 62 | 71 | 75 | 72 | 70 |
| Experiment 2 (iron): temperature / °C | 21 | 25 | 32 | 38 | 41 | 43 | 44 |

**a** Plot **two** graphs on the grid provided and label each with the name of the metal.

**b** Write the word equation for the first reaction and the balanced symbol equation for the second.

..................................................................................................................................................

..................................................................................................................................................

**c** Which metal, iron or zinc, produced the larger temperature rise?

..................................................................................................................................................

**d** Suggest why this metal gave the larger temperature rise.

..................................................................................................................................................

..................................................................................................................................................

**e** Comment on whether this experiment is a 'fair test'. Explain your answer.

..................................................................................................................................................

..................................................................................................................................................

..................................................................................................................................................

Use the checklist below to give yourself a mark for your graph.

For each point, award yourself:

2 marks if you did it really well

1 mark if you made a good attempt at it, and partly succeeded

0 marks if you did not try to do it, or did not succeed.

**Self-assessment checklist for graphs:**

| Check point | Marks awarded | |
| --- | --- | --- |
| | You | Your teacher |
| You have drawn the axes with a ruler, using most of the width and height of the grid. | | |
| You have used a good scale for the $x$-axis and the $y$-axis, going up in useful proportions. | | |
| You have labelled the axes correctly, giving the correct units for the scales on both axes. | | |
| You have plotted each point precisely and correctly. | | |
| You have used a small, neat dot or cross for each point. | | |
| You have drawn a single, clear best-fit line through each set of points – using a ruler for a straight line. | | |
| You have ignored any anomalous results when drawing the lines through each set of results. | | |
| **Total (out of 14)** | | |

12–14  Excellent.

10–11  Good.

7–9  A good start, but you need to improve quite a bit.

5–6  Poor. Try this same graph again, using a new sheet of graph paper.

1–4  Very poor. Read through all the criteria again, and then try the same graph again.

## Generating electrical energy

In these metal displacement reactions, the atoms of the reactive metal lose electrons to become ions. For example:

$$Zn(s) \rightarrow Zn^{2+}(aq) + 2e^-$$

**f**  Is this reduction or oxidation? .............................

The electrons produced are given to the metal ion in solution to form an atom of the displaced metal.

$$Cu^{2+}(aq) + 2e^- \rightarrow Cu(s)$$

**s** In an electrochemical cell, these electrons are sent through a circuit to produce an electrical current. The flow of electrons is from the more reactive metal (zinc) to the less reactive metal (copper).

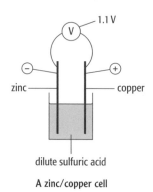

A zinc/copper cell

The voltage produced is a measure of the difference in reactivity of the two metals. A copper/iron cell produces a different voltage.

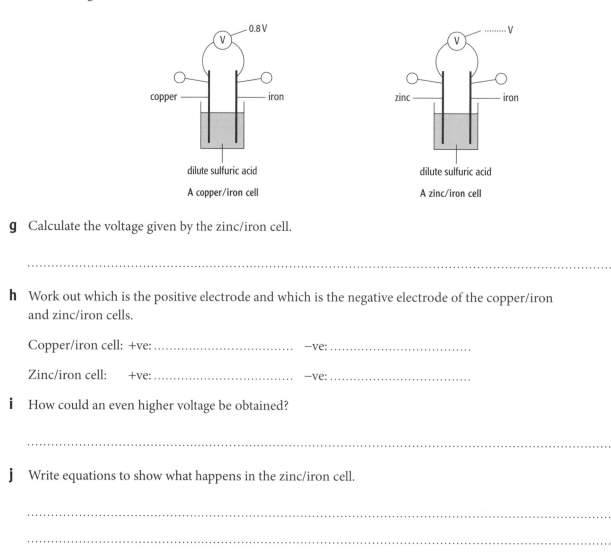

**g** Calculate the voltage given by the zinc/iron cell.

.................................................................................................................................................................

**h** Work out which is the positive electrode and which is the negative electrode of the copper/iron and zinc/iron cells.

Copper/iron cell:  +ve:.................................... −ve:....................................

Zinc/iron cell:    +ve:.................................... −ve:....................................

**i** How could an even higher voltage be obtained?

.................................................................................................................................................................

**j** Write equations to show what happens in the zinc/iron cell.

.................................................................................................................................................................

.................................................................................................................................................................

# Exercise 8.4    Electrochemical cells

This exercise examines the design of electrochemical cells and is aimed at making you more confident in your understanding of the components of these cells.

a  Electrochemical cells are based on the difference in reactivity between the metals that form the electrodes of the cell. The diagram below shows one of the earliest forms of cell (the Daniel cell).

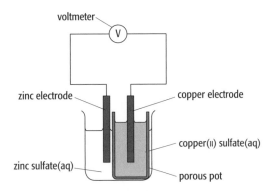

The reaction taking place at the right-hand electrode is: $Cu^{2+}(aq) + 2e^- \rightarrow Cu(s)$

i    Does this reaction represent oxidation or reduction? Explain your answer.

    ....................................................................................................................................................................

    ....................................................................................................................................................................

ii   Write the half-equation for the reaction taking place at the zinc electrode. Include state symbols in the equation.

    ....................................................................................................................................................................

iii  Which way do electrons flow around the circuit? Explain your reasoning. What would be the charges on the two electrodes?

    ....................................................................................................................................................................

    ....................................................................................................................................................................

    Charge on the zinc electrode: ...........................................................................

    Charge on the copper electrode: ...........................................................................

iv   What carries the electric current through the solutions?

    ....................................................................................................................................................................

v    What is the purpose of the porous pot?

    ....................................................................................................................................................................

**vi** The high-resistance voltmeter measures the voltage of the cell. What would happen to the voltage produced if the zinc electrode were replaced by magnesium? Explain your answer.

.......................................................................................................................................................

.......................................................................................................................................................

The terms **anode** and **cathode** are applied to the electrodes of any cell as follows:

- The anode is the electrode at which oxidation takes place.
- The cathode is the electrode at which reduction takes place.

**vii** State which electrode is the anode and which is the cathode in the cell illustrated on the previous page.

Zinc electrode: .....................................................

Copper electrode: .....................................................

**viii** What observations can be made regarding the sizes of the two electrodes as the cell is being used? Explain the observations in terms of the reactions taking place at the electrodes.

Zinc electrode

.......................................................................................................................................................

.......................................................................................................................................................

.......................................................................................................................................................

Copper electrode

.......................................................................................................................................................

.......................................................................................................................................................

.......................................................................................................................................................

**b** A student measured the voltage produced by four cells. Two of the results are shown in the table below.

| Cell number | Metal A | Metal B | Voltage / volts |
|:-----------:|---------|---------|:---------------:|
| 1 | iron | copper | 0.8 |
| 2 | magnesium | copper | 2.7 |
| 3 | copper | copper | |
| 4 | zinc | copper | |

**i** Complete the last two lines of the right-hand column in the table by selecting from the following list of voltages:

3.4        1.1        0.3        0.0

**ii** State **two** factors which must remain the same in all the experiments if the comparison of the voltages is to be fair.

.................................................................................................................................................

.................................................................................................................................................

**iii** Name **two** metals which could safely be used to give a value greater than 2.7 volts if they were connected together in a similar cell.

.................................................................................................................................................

# Exercise 8.5   Metals and alloys

> This exercise discusses some aspects of alloys and their usefulness. It explores the advantages and specific purpose of certain alloys.

The table shows some properties of a selection of pure metals.

| Metal | Relative abundance in Earth's crust | Cost of extraction | Density | Strength | Melting point/°C | Electrical conductivity relative to iron |
|---|---|---|---|---|---|---|
| iron | 2nd | low | high | high | 1535 | 1.0 |
| titanium | 7th | very high | low | high | 1660 | 0.2 |
| aluminium | 1st | high | low | medium | 660 | 3.5 |
| zinc | 19th | low | high | low | 419 | 1.7 |
| copper | 20th | low | high | medium | 1083 | 6.0 |
| tin | 40th | low | high | low | 231 | 0.9 |
| lead | 30th | low | very high | low | 327 | 0.5 |

Use information from the table to answer the following questions.

**a** Why is aluminium used for overhead power cables?

.................................................................................................................................................

**b** Why do the aluminium cables have an iron (or steel) core?

.................................................................................................................................................

**c** Why is copper used instead of aluminium in wiring in the home?

.................................................................................................................................................

**d** Why is titanium a good metal to use for jet aircraft and Formula 1 racing cars?

.................................................................................................................................................

.................................................................................................................................................

Alloys have different properties from the metals they are made from. They are usually harder and stronger with lower melting points.

**e** **Solder**, which is melted to join together electrical components on circuit boards is a mixture of tin and lead. Suggest why it is used in preference to the pure metals.

.................................................................................................................................................

.................................................................................................................................................

**f** **Brass** is an alloy of copper and zinc. It is used to make brass musical instruments and to make electrical connectors and plugs.

There are two main types of brass: 60:40 and 70:30 copper to zinc. The larger the amount of zinc, the harder and stronger the alloy is.

Suggest which alloy is used for each of the purposes mentioned above. Give a reason for your answers.

Cu60:Zn40

.................................................................................................................................................

.................................................................................................................................................

Cu70:Zn30

.................................................................................................................................................

.................................................................................................................................................

# 9 Industrial inorganic chemistry

## Definitions to learn

- **chemical plant** the reaction vessels and equipment for manufacturing chemicals
- **feedstock** starting materials for chemical industrial processes
- **brine** a concentrated solution of sodium chloride
- **Haber process** the industrial process for the manufacture of ammonia
- **Contact process** the industrial process for the manufacture of sulfuric acid

## Useful equations

$Fe_2O_3 + 3CO \rightarrow 2Fe + 3CO_2$      blast furnace reaction

$CaCO_3 \rightarrow CaO + CO_2$      lime kiln reaction

$Al^{3+}(l) + 3e^- \rightarrow Al(l)$      extraction of aluminium

$N_2(g) + 3H_2(g) \rightleftharpoons 2NH_3(g)$      Haber process

$2SO_2(g) + O_2(g) \rightleftharpoons 2SO_3(g)$      Contact process

## Exercise 9.1   Metal alloys and their uses

This exercise should help you recall details of different alloys and the basis of their usefulness.

Complete the following table about the composition and usefulness of some alloys by filling in the gaps.

| Alloy | Composition | Use | Useful property |
|---|---|---|---|
| mild steel | iron: > 99.75%<br>carbon: < 0.25% | ........................... | ........................... |
| stainless steel | iron: 74%<br>........................... : 18%<br>nickel: 8% | ..........................., surgical instruments, chemical vessels for industry | ........................... |
| brass | copper: 70%<br>........................... : 30% | ........................... instruments, ornaments | 'gold' colour, harder than copper |
| bronze | copper: 95%<br>........................... : 5% | statues, church bells | hard, does not ........................... |

*(Continued)*

| Alloy | Composition | Use | Useful property |
|---|---|---|---|
| aerospace aluminium | aluminium: 90.25% zinc: 6% magnesium: 2.5% copper: 1.25% | aircraft construction | ............................ |
| solder | tin: 60% lead: 40% | ............................ | low melting point |
| tungsten steel | iron: 95% tungsten: 5% | cutting edges of drill bits | ............................ |

## Ⓢ Exercise 9.2  Extracting aluminium by electrolysis

> This exercise should help you recall and understand the details of the method for extracting aluminium.

Because of its high reactivity, aluminium must be extracted by electrolysis. The electrolyte is aluminium oxide dissolved in molten cryolite. Hydrated aluminium oxide is heated to produce the pure aluminium oxide used.

$$Al_2O_3 \cdot 3H_2O \quad \rightarrow \quad Al_2O_3 + 3H_2O$$
hydrated aluminium oxide

**a**  What type of reaction is this? Put a ring around the correct answer.

**decomposition**       **neutralisation**       **oxidation**       **reduction**

**b**  Why must the electrolyte be molten for electrolysis to occur?

.............................................................................................................................................................

**c**  What is the purpose of the cryolite?

.............................................................................................................................................................

**d**  In the following diagram of the electrolysis cell, which letter (**A**, **B**, **C** or **D**) represents the cathode? ..........

**e**  State the name of the products formed at the anode and cathode during this electrolysis.

At the anode: ..................................... At the cathode: .....................................

**f** Why do the anodes have to be renewed periodically?

..............................................................................................................................................................

**g** Complete the equation for the formation of aluminium from aluminium ions.

$Al^{3+} + ............... e^- \rightarrow Al$

**h** State **one** use of aluminium.

..............................................................................................................................................................

## Exercise 9.3 The importance of nitrogen *please complete the assignment.*

> The following exercise connects the ideas surrounding the importance of nitrogen to agriculture and develops your understanding of chemical equilibria. It also develops your skills in processing and interpreting experimental results.

Although certain bacteria in the soil convert nitrogen gas into nitrates, other bacteria convert nitrogen into ammonium salts. The ionic equation for this second reaction is:

$N_2 + 8H^+ + 6e^- \rightarrow 2NH_4^+$

**a** Explain why this is a reduction reaction.

..............................................................................................................................................................

**b** In the presence of hydrogen ions, bacteria of a different type convert nitrate ions into nitrogen gas and water. Give the ionic equation for this reaction.

..............................................................................................................................................................

Ammonia is made by the Haber process using an iron catalyst.

$$N_2 + 3H_2 \rightleftharpoons 2NH_3 \quad \text{(the forward reaction is exothermic)}$$

The raw materials for the Haber process can be obtained from the air and from natural gas.

**c** What method is used to separate pure nitrogen from other gases in the air?

..............................................................................................................................................................

**d** Describe how hydrogen can be made from hydrocarbons.

..............................................................................................................................................................

..............................................................................................................................................................

**e** State the essential conditions of temperature and pressure used for the Haber process.

..................................................................................................................................................................

**f** Sketch an energy profile diagram to show both the catalysed and the uncatalysed reaction. Label the diagram to show the following key features: the reactants and products, the enthalpy change for the reaction, and the catalysed and uncatalysed reactions.

The table shows how the percentage of ammonia in the mixture leaving the reaction vessel varies under different conditions.

| Pressure / atm | 100 | 200 | 300 | 400 |
|---|---|---|---|---|
| % of ammonia at 300 °C | 45 | 65 | 72 | 78 |
| % of ammonia at 500 °C | 9 | 18 | 25 | 31 |

**g** Use the grid to plot graphs of the percentage of ammonia against pressure at both 300 °C and 500 °C.

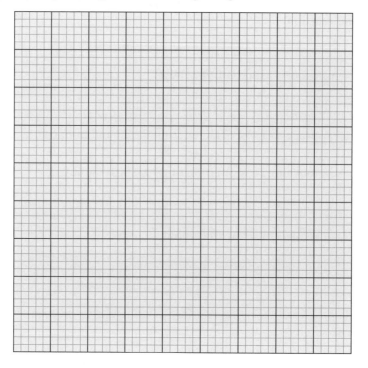

Use the checklist below to give yourself a mark for your graph.

For each point, award yourself:

2 marks if you did it really well

1 mark if you made a good attempt at it, and partly succeeded

0 marks if you did not try to do it, or did not succeed.

**Self-assessment checklist for graphs:**

| Check point | Marks awarded | |
| --- | --- | --- |
| | You | Your teacher |
| You have drawn the axes with a ruler, using most of the width and height of the grid. | | |
| You have used a good scale for the *x*-axis and the *y*-axis, going up in useful proportions. | | |
| You have labelled the axes correctly, giving the correct units for the scales on both axes. | | |
| You have plotted each point precisely and correctly. | | |
| You have used a small, neat dot or cross for each point. | | |
| You have drawn a single, clear best-fit line through each set of points – using a ruler for any straight line. | | |
| You have ignored any anomalous results when drawing the line. | | |
| Total (out of 14) | | |

12–14   Excellent.

10–11   Good.

7–9     A good start, but you need to improve quite a bit.

5–6     Poor. Try this same graph again, using a new sheet of graph paper.

1–4     Very poor. Read through all the criteria again, and then try the same graph again.

**h**   What is the percentage of ammonia formed at 250 atmospheres and 300 °C?

.................................................................................................................................................................................................

**i**   Use your graphs to estimate the percentage of ammonia formed at 400 °C and 250 atmospheres.

.................................................................................................................................................................................................

**j**   The advantage of using a low temperature is the large percentage of ammonia formed. What is the disadvantage of using a low temperature?

.................................................................................................................................................................................................

**s** **k** Suggest **two** advantages of using high pressure in the manufacture of ammonia.

..........................................................................................................................................................

..........................................................................................................................................................

The most important use of ammonia is in fertiliser production. Fertilisers are added to the soil to improve crop yields. A farmer has the choice of two fertilisers, ammonium nitrate, $NH_4NO_3$, or diammonium hydrogen phosphate, $(NH_4)_2HPO_4$.

**l** Show by calculation which of these fertilisers contains the greater percentage of nitrogen by mass.

**m** State **one** major problem caused when the nitrates from fertilisers leach from the soil into streams and rivers.

..........................................................................................................................................................

## Exercise 9.4    Making sulfuric acid industrially

> This exercise helps your understanding of chemical equilibria, particularly the factors involved in the Contact process.

The diagram shows the three different stages in the manufacture of sulfuric acid.

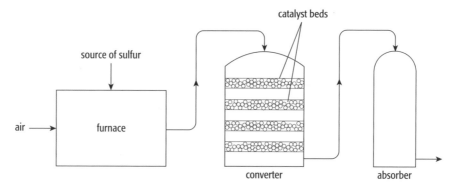

One possible source of sulfur is an ore containing zinc sulfide, ZnS. In the furnace, this sulfide ore is heated in oxygen to make zinc oxide, ZnO, and sulfur dioxide.

**a** Write an equation for this reaction.

..........................................................................................................................................................

**5** In the converter, sulfur dioxide and oxygen are passed over a series of catalyst beds at a temperature of about 420 °C.

$$2SO_2(g) + O_2(g) \rightleftharpoons 2SO_3(g) \qquad \Delta H = -196\,kJ$$

**b** An increase in pressure increases the yield of sulfur trioxide. Explain the reason for this effect.

.................................................................................................................................................

.................................................................................................................................................

**c** Even though an increase in pressure increases the yield of sulfur trioxide, the reaction in the converter is carried out at atmospheric pressure. Suggest a reason for this.

.................................................................................................................................................

.................................................................................................................................................

**d** In some sulfuric acid plants, the gases are cooled when they pass from one catalyst bed to the next. Use the information given about the nature of the reaction to explain why the gases need to be cooled.

.................................................................................................................................................

.................................................................................................................................................

# Exercise 9.5 Concrete chemistry

> This exercise will aid your recall of the important uses of limestone and help your familiarity with questions asked in an unusual context.

Limestone is an important mineral resource. One use is in the making of cement. Cement is made by heating clay with crushed limestone. During this process, the calcium carbonate is first converted to calcium oxide.

$$CaCO_3 \rightarrow CaO + CO_2$$

**a** What name is given to this type of chemical reaction?

*decomposition reaction*

Concrete is then made from cement, sand and water. When it has set, concrete is slightly porous. Rainwater can soak into concrete and some of the unreacted calcium oxide present dissolves to form calcium hydroxide.

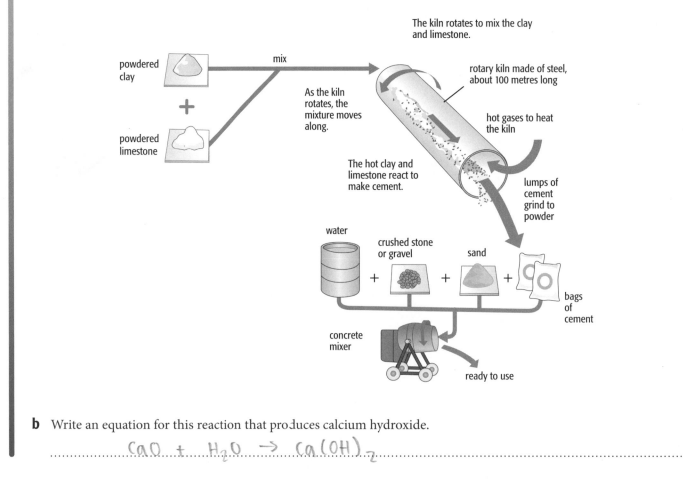

The kiln rotates to mix the clay and limestone.

powdered clay

+

powdered limestone

mix

As the kiln rotates, the mixture moves along.

rotary kiln made of steel, about 100 metres long

hot gases to heat the kiln

The hot clay and limestone react to make cement.

lumps of cement grind to powder

water

crushed stone or gravel

sand

bags of cement

concrete mixer

ready to use

**b** Write an equation for this reaction that produces calcium hydroxide.

$$CaO + H_2O \rightarrow Ca(OH)_2$$

**S** The aqueous calcium hydroxide in wet concrete is able to react with carbon dioxide in the air.

$$Ca(OH)_2 + CO_2 \rightarrow CaCO_3 + H_2O$$

The diagram shows how the pH can vary at different points inside a cracked concrete beam.

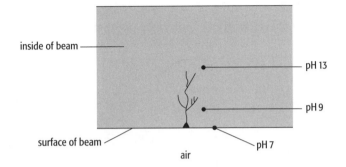

**c** Describe the change in pH from the surface to the centre of the beam, and explain why this variation occurs.

The surface touches more air so more cement is neutralized. As it goes to the center of the beam, less air is present, so the cement can't neutralize and remains alkaline.

**d** Describe briefly two other uses for limestone in addition to making cement.

It is used to neutralise acidic soils and lakes and used to manufacture glass.

# Exercise 9.6   The chlor–alkali industry

> This exercise is concerned with the industrial electrolysis of brine and emphasises the usefulness and wide range of the products formed by this process.

The electrolysis of brine is arguably one of the most efficient industrial processes. This stems from the fact that all of the major products act as the starting points for the manufacture of other useful chemicals. There is essentially no waste product from the process.

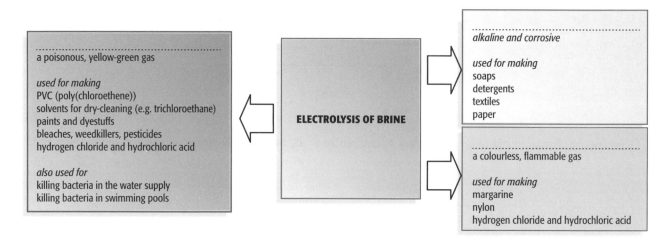

**a**   The starting point for this industrial process is a concentrated brine solution.

   **i**   What is **brine**?

   ......................................................................................................................................................

   **ii**   What are the **three** major products of the electrolysis of brine? List them below and write their names in on the diagram above

   ......................................................................................................................................................

**b**   Two of the products of the electrolysis can be reacted together to produce sodium chlorate(ɪ) and sodium chlorate(v). These are commercial products that are sold as bleach and weedkiller respectively.

   **i**   Complete the following word equation for the production of sodium chlorate(ɪ).

   ...........................+.........................→     sodium     +     sodium     +     water
   ...........................                                 chlorate(ɪ)          chloride

   **ii**   Sodium chlorate(ɪ) is used as a bleach but also as a treatment for the domestic water supply and swimming pools. What is the purpose of this treatment?

   ......................................................................................................................................................

   **iii**   Sodium chlorate(v) is an ionic compound made up of sodium ions and chlorate(v) ions ($ClO_3^-$). What is the formula of sodium chlorate(v)?

   ......................................................................................................................................................

**iv** The two gases produced in the electrolysis of brine can be reacted together to form hydrogen chloride. Write the word and balanced symbol equations for this reaction.

.................................................................................................................................................

.................................................................................................................................................

**c** The membrane cell for the electrolysis of brine is shown in the following diagram.

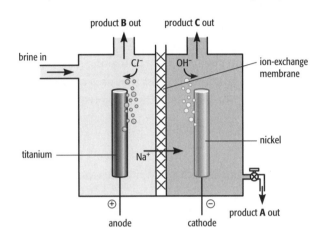

**i** What is the purpose of the membrane in the electrolysis cell?

.................................................................................................................................................

.................................................................................................................................................

**ii** Why is the anode made of titanium?

.................................................................................................................................................

**iii** Write the half-equations for the reactions taking place at the anode and cathode. Include state symbols in your equations.

At the anode: ...................................................................................................

At the cathode: ...................................................................................................

**d** Chlorine is reacted with various hydrocarbons to produce useful solvents. For example, chlorine reacts with ethene to produce 1,2-dichloroethane.

**i** What type of reaction is this?

.................................................................................................................................................

**ii** What is the structural formula of 1,2-dichloroethane?

# Exercise 9.7 Making sodium carbonate

> This exercise discusses the nature and recycling of industrial raw materials in the novel context of the Solvay process for the manufacture of sodium carbonate.

All chemical industries depend on the availability of suitable starting materials. The chlor–alkali industry discussed in the previous exercise is often located close to underground deposits of salt. Another industrial process that uses salt as a feedstock is the Solvay process for the production of sodium carbonate.

**a** Sodium carbonate, $Na_2CO_3$, is an important chemical used in making glass, soaps, detergents, paper, dyes and other chemicals. It is manufactured in a continuous process that uses carbon dioxide and ammonia dissolved in brine as its starting materials. The Solvay process for making it involves two steps:

step 1: $NaCl + H_2O + NH_3 + CO_2 \rightarrow NH_4Cl + NaHCO_3$
step 2: $2NaHCO_3 \rightarrow Na_2CO_3 + CO_2 + H_2O$

**i** The carbon dioxide is obtained by heating limestone. Write the word and symbol equations for this thermal decomposition.

.................................................................................................................................................

.................................................................................................................................................

.................................................................................................................................................

**ii** By considering the equations for the two steps, deduce how many moles of sodium carbonate could be made from 100 moles of sodium chloride.

.................................................................................................................................................

.................................................................................................................................................

**iii** How many tonnes of sodium carbonate could be obtained from 100 moles of sodium chloride?

.................................................................................................................................................

.................................................................................................................................................

.................................................................................................................................................

**iv** What would be the percentage yield of the process if 1.59 kg of sodium carbonate were obtained from 100 moles of sodium chloride?

.................................................................................................................................................

.................................................................................................................................................

.................................................................................................................................................

**b** The Solvay process is economical because it involves the recycling of starting materials. Consider the equations for the two steps of the process again.

**i** Which gas can clearly be recycled between the two steps?

.................................................................................................................................................

**ii** In fact, the ammonia used in the process can also be recycled. The ammonium chloride formed during step **2** can be heated with calcium oxide made from heating limestone.

Complete the equation for the formation of ammonia.

$2NH_4Cl$    +    $CaO$    →    ................    +    $CaCl_2$    +    ................

**iii** Calcium chloride is a by-product of the Solvay process. It is sold for treating roads in winter. Why is this salt spread on roads in winter?

.................................................................................................................................................................

.................................................................................................................................................................

# 10 Organic chemistry

## Definitions to learn

- **hydrocarbon** a compound that contains carbon and hydrogen only
- **saturated hydrocarbon** a hydrocarbon that contains only single covalent bonds between the carbon atoms
- **alkane** a saturated hydrocarbon that contains only single covalent bonds between the carbon atoms of the chain; the simplest alkane is methane, $CH_4$
- **alkene** an unsaturated hydrocarbon that contains at least one double bond between two of the carbon atoms in the chain; the simplest alkene is ethene, $C_2H_4$
- **homologous series** a family of organic compounds with similar chemical properties as they contain the same functional group; alkenes, alcohols, for instance
- **isomers** molecules with the same molecular formula but different structural formulae
- **substitution reaction** a reaction in which one or more hydrogen atoms in a hydrocarbon are replaced by atoms of another element
- **addition reaction** a reaction in which atoms, or groups, are added across a carbon–carbon double bond in an unsaturated molecule such as an alkene

## Useful equations

$$CH_4 + 2O_2 \rightarrow CO_2 + 2H_2O$$
methane + oxygen → carbon dioxide + water

burning methane

$$C_2H_5OH + 3O_2 \rightarrow 2CO_2 + 3H_2O$$
ethanol + oxygen → carbon dioxide + water

burning ethanol

$$C_6H_{12}O_6 \rightarrow 2C_2H_5OH + 2CO_2$$
glucose → ethanol + carbon dioxide

fermentation

$$CH_4 + Cl_2 \rightarrow CH_3Cl + HCl$$
methane + chlorine → chloromethane + hydrogen chloride

substitution

$$C_2H_5OH + 2[O] \rightarrow CH_3COOH + H_2O$$
ethanol + [oxygen] → ethanoic acid + water

oxidation

$$C_2H_5OH + CH_3COOH \rightleftharpoons CH_3COOC_2H_5 + H_2O$$
ethanol + ethanoic acid ⇌ ethyl ethanoate + water

esterification

# Exercise 10.1  Families of hydrocarbons

> This exercise helps you revise the key features of the families of hydrocarbons and develops your understanding of the structures of organic compounds.

**a**  Complete the passage using only words from the list.

~~bromine~~   ~~alkanes~~   ~~hydrogen~~   ~~double~~   chlorine   ~~chains~~   ~~petroleum~~
~~methane~~   ~~ethene~~   ethane   ~~colourless~~   propane   ~~alkenes~~

The chief source of organic compounds is the naturally occurring mixture of hydrocarbons known as

..... _petroleum_ ........... . Hydrocarbons are compounds that contain carbon and ..... _hydrogen_ ...........

only. There are many hydrocarbons because of the ability of carbon atoms to join together to form long

.......... _chains_ ............. . There is a series of hydrocarbons with just single covalent bonds between the carbon

atoms in the molecule. These are saturated hydrocarbons, and they are called ...... _alkanes_ ............... . The

simplest of these saturated hydrocarbons has the formula $CH_4$ and is called ...... _methane_ ............ . Unsaturated

hydrocarbons can also occur. These molecules contain at least one carbon–carbon ........ _double_ ........... bond.

These compounds belong to the ........... _alkenes_ ......., a second series of hydrocarbons. The simplest of this

'family' of unsaturated hydrocarbons has the formula $C_2H_4$ and is known as .......... _ethene_ ............. .

The test for an unsaturated hydrocarbon is to add the sample to ........ _bromine_ ........... water. It changes colour

from orange/brown to ........ _colourless_ ....... if the hydrocarbon is unsaturated.

**b**  The table shows the names, formulae and boiling points of the first members of the homologous series of unsaturated hydrocarbons. Complete the table by filling in the spaces.

| Name | Formula | Boiling point / °C |
|---|---|---|
| _ethene_ | $C_2H_4$ | −102 |
| propene | $C_3H_6$ | −48 |
| butene | $C_4H_8$ | −7 |
| pentene | $C_5H_{10}$ | 30 |
| hexene | $C_6H_{12}$ | 63 |

**c**  Deduce the molecular formula of the alkene which has a relative molecular mass of 168.

...................................................................................................................................

# Exercise 10.2 Unsaturated hydrocarbons (the alkenes)

> This exercise develops your understanding of unsaturated hydrocarbons using an unfamiliar example.

Limonene is a colourless unsaturated hydrocarbon found in oranges and lemons. The structure of limonene is shown here.

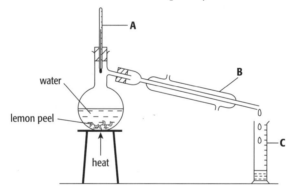

**a** On the structure, draw a circle around the bonds which make limonene an unsaturated hydrocarbon.

**b** What is the molecular formula of limonene?

...........$C_{10}H_{16}$............................................................................................

**c** Describe the colour change which occurs when excess limonene is added to a few drops of bromine water.

............It will turn colorless.................................................................................

The diagram shows how limonene can be extracted from lemon peel by steam distillation.

**d** State the name of the pieces of apparatus labelled **A**, **B** and **C**.

A..........thermometer..........B..........condenser..........C..graduated cylinder

When limonene undergoes incomplete combustion, carbon monoxide is formed.

**e** What do you understand by the term **incomplete combustion**?

......Incomplete combustion is the burning of fuels in a limited supply.....
....of oxygen; It gives carbon monoxide instead of carbon dioxide.....

**f** State an adverse effect of carbon monoxide on health.

......Carbon monoxide causes harmful health effects, it can reduce......
....oxygen delivery to the body's organs (heart and brain).....

**g** The structures of some compounds found in plants are shown below.

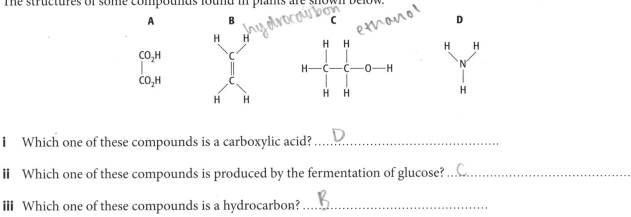

*(handwritten labels: B "hydrocarbon", C "ethanol")*

  **i** Which one of these compounds is a carboxylic acid? .....D..........................................

  **ii** Which one of these compounds is produced by the fermentation of glucose? ...C..................................

  **iii** Which one of these compounds is a hydrocarbon? .....B........................................

**h** All hydrocarbons are covalently bonded whether saturated or unsaturated. Draw 'dot-and-cross' diagrams for methane and ethane illustrating the arrangement of the bonding electrons. You only need to draw the outer electrons of the carbon atoms.

Methane :

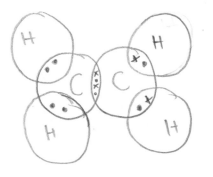

CH$_4$

Ethane :

C$_2$H$_4$

# Exercise 10.3   The alcohols as fuels

> The following exercise uses information relating to the alcohols to develop your understanding of these compounds and to enhance your presentation, analysis and interpretation of experimental data concerning their property as fuels.

The table shows the formulae of the first three members of the alcohol homologous series.

| Alcohol | Formula |
|---------|---------|
| methanol | $CH_3OH$ |
| ethanol | $C_2H_5OH$ |
| propanol | $C_3H_7OH$ |

**a**  Use the information given to deduce the general formula for the alcohol homologous series.

..........................................................................................................................................................

Ethanol, the most significant of the alcohols, can be manufactured from either ethene or glucose.

**b**  Write an equation for the industrial production of ethanol from ethene and state the conditions under which the reaction takes place.

..........................................................................................................................................................

..........................................................................................................................................................

The fermentation (anaerobic respiration) of glucose by yeast can be represented by the following equation. The reaction is catalysed by the enzyme zymase. After a few days, the reaction stops. It has produced a 12% aqueous solution of ethanol.

$$C_6H_{12}O_6 \rightarrow 2C_2H_5OH + 2CO_2$$

**c**  Sketch a labelled diagram to show how fermentation can be carried out.

**d**  Suggest a reason why the reaction stops after a few days.

..........................................................................................................................................................

..........................................................................................................................................................

**e** Why is it essential that there is no oxygen in the reaction vessel?

..............................................................................................................................................

..............................................................................................................................................

**f** Name the products of the complete combustion of ethanol.

..............................................................................................................................................

**g** Explain why ethanol made from ethene is a non-renewable fuel, but that made from glucose is a renewable fuel.

..............................................................................................................................................

..............................................................................................................................................

..............................................................................................................................................

A student used this apparatus to investigate the amount of heat produced when ethanol was burnt.

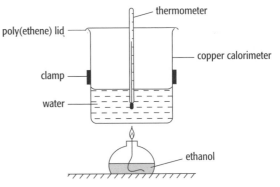

**h** Draw the structure of ethanol showing all atoms and bonds.

**i** Complete the equation for the complete combustion of ethanol.

$$C_2H_5OH + 3O_2 \rightarrow \text{...............} CO_2 + \text{................} H_2O$$

**j** When 2.3 g of ethanol are burnt, 2.7 g of water are formed. Calculate the mass of water formed when 13.8 g of ethanol are burnt.

The experiment was later adapted to compare the heat released by burning four different alcohols. Each burner in turn was weighed and then the alcohol was allowed to burn until the temperature of the water had risen by 15 °C. The flame was then extinguished and the burner re-weighed. The results obtained are shown on the following page.

| Alcohol | Formula | Mass of alcohol burnt / g |
|---|---|---|
| methanol | $CH_3OH$ | 0.90 |
| ethanol | $C_2H_5OH$ | 0.70 |
| propan-1-ol | $C_3H_7OH$ | 0.62 |
| pentan-1-ol | $C_5H_{11}OH$ | 0.57 |

**k** Plot a graph showing how the mass of alcohol required varies with the number of carbon atoms in the alcohol used. Draw a smooth curve through the points.

Use the checklist below to give yourself a mark for your graph.
For each point, award yourself:
2 marks if you did it really well
1 mark if you made a good attempt at it, and partly succeeded
0 marks if you did not try to do it, or did not succeed.

**Self-assessment checklist for graphs:**

| Check point | Marks awarded | |
|---|---|---|
| | You | Your teacher |
| You have drawn the axes with a ruler, using most of the width and height of the grid. | | |
| You have used a good scale for the x-axis and the y-axis, going up in useful proportions. | | |
| You have labelled the axes correctly, giving the correct units for the scales on both axes. | | |
| You have plotted each point precisely and correctly. | | |
| You have used a small, neat cross or dot for each point. | | |
| You have drawn a single, clear best-fit line through the points. | | |
| You have ignored any anomalous results when drawing the line. | | |
| Total (out of 14) | | |

12–14   Excellent.
10–11   Good.
7–9     A good start, but you need to improve quite a bit.
5–6     Poor. Try this same graph again, using a new sheet of graph paper.
1–4     Very poor. Read through all the criteria again, and then try the same graph again.

**l** Predict the mass of butanol, $C_4H_9OH$, which, on combustion, would raise the temperature of the water by 15 °C.

..............................................................................................................................................

**m** Suggest a reason why the same temperature rise (15 °C) was used in each experiment.

..............................................................................................................................................

..............................................................................................................................................

**S** **n** One student found a different value of 0.66 g for the mass of propanol burnt in this experiment. This student had accidentally used a different isomer of propanol. Give the name and structure of this isomer.

Name: ......................................

Structure

# Exercise 10.4  Reactions of ethanoic acid

> This exercise revises some aspects of the chemistry of carboxylic acids.

Acidified potassium dichromate(VI) was used to oxidise ethanol to ethanoic acid using the apparatus in the diagram.

**a** Which of the following best describes the purpose of the condenser set up as shown? Put a ring around the correct answer.

  **A** to prevent the conversion of ethanoic acid back to ethanol

  **B** to prevent condensation of the oxidising agent

  **C** to prevent escape of the unreacted alcohol

  **D** to prevent reaction between ethanol and ethanoic acid

water out

condenser

water in

ethanol and acidified potassium dichromate(VI)

heat

**b** Ethanoic acid, $CH_3CO_2H$, is a weak acid. Explain what is meant by the term **weak acid**.

..............................................................................................................................................

..............................................................................................................................................

**c** Ethanoic acid reacts with sodium carbonate. Write the equation for this reaction.

..............................................................................................................................................................

Ethanoic acid also reacts with magnesium to form magnesium ethanoate and hydrogen.

$$Mg + 2CH_3CO_2H \rightarrow (CH_3CO_2)_2Mg + H_2$$

A student added 4.80 g of magnesium to 25.0 g of ethanoic acid. (Note the relative atomic masses H = 1, C = 12, O = 16 and Mg = 24, and that the molar volume of a gas = 24 $dm^3$ at r.t.p.)

**d** Which of the reactants, magnesium or ethanoic acid, is used in excess in this experiment? Explain your answer.

..............................................................................................................................................................

..............................................................................................................................................................

..............................................................................................................................................................

..............................................................................................................................................................

**e** Calculate both the number of moles of hydrogen and the volume of hydrogen that would be formed at r.t.p.

# Exercise 10.5 Hydrocarbons and their reactions

> This exercise is aimed at developing your confidence in discussing aspects of the chemistry of the hydrocarbons, particularly their use as fuels.

**a** Complete the following table. (Relative atomic masses: H = 1, C = 12.)

| Name of hydrocarbon | ethane | ethene |
|---|---|---|
| Molecular formula of hydrocarbon | $C_2H_6$ | |
| Relative molecular mass of hydrocarbon | | |
| Structural formula of hydrocarbon | | |
| Colour of bromine water after being shaken with the hydrocarbon | | colourless |

**b** The hydrocarbon propane is an important constituent of the fuel liquid petroleum gas (LPG). For the burning of propane in an excess of air, give:

**i** a word equation

.................................................................................................................................

**ii** a balanced symbol equation.

.................................................................................................................................

**iii** Use your answer to give the number of moles of water formed when one mole of propane is burnt in an excess of air.

.................................................................................................................................

**c** Bromine reacts with alkanes in a similar way to chlorine. Hydrogen bromide is made in the substitution reaction between propane and bromine:

propane + bromine → bromopropane + hydrogen bromide

**i** Draw the structure of propane.

**ii** Draw the structure of a bromopropane.

**iii** The reaction between propane and bromine is photochemical. Suggest what is meant by **photochemical**.

.................................................................................................................................................

.................................................................................................................................................

**d** Butane is the alkane which contains four carbon atoms in each molecule.

  **i** Draw the structural formula of butane and of an isomer of butane.

  **ii** When butane is burnt, the following reaction takes place:

$$2C_4H_{10} + 13O_2 \rightarrow 8CO_2 + 10H_2O$$

  • How many moles of butane have to be burnt to produce four moles of carbon dioxide?

.................................................................................................................................................

  • Calculate the mass of one mole of butane ($C_4H_{10}$).

.................................................................................................................................................

  • Calculate the mass of one mole of carbon dioxide.

.................................................................................................................................................

  • How many grams of carbon dioxide would be produced if 5.8 g of butane were burnt?

.................................................................................................................................................

.................................................................................................................................................

**e** Unsaturated hydrocarbons take part in addition reactions.

  **i** Write a word equation for the reaction between propene and hydrogen.

.................................................................................................................................................

  **ii** Write a symbol equation for the reaction between butene and steam.

.................................................................................................................................................

**f** A major use of LPG is in various forms of bottled gas. This gas which can be used for barbecues and domestic and patio heaters involves using propane and/or butane under pressure in canisters.

  **i** Carry out an internet search to find out which of these gases gives the most heat for a given mass of gas.

.................................................................................................................................................

.................................................................................................................................................

.................................................................................................................................................

.................................................................................................................................................

**ii** For bottled mixtures of LPG, the proportions of propane and butane in the mixture are changed seasonally. One gas is preferred in the winter, the other in summer. Research the nature of this preference and why it is made.

..........................................................................................................................................

..........................................................................................................................................

..........................................................................................................................................

..........................................................................................................................................

## ⓢ Exercise 10.6   The chemistry of butanol

> This exercise explores aspects of the chemistry of butan-1-ol and related compounds. It also discusses the use of butan-1-ol as a biofuel.

Butan-1-ol is an increasingly important alcohol which can be made in the laboratory and in industry in a variety of different ways. Industrially, it can then be used as a solvent for paints and varnishes, to make esters and as a fuel.

**a** In the laboratory, 1-chlorobutane can be reacted with sodium hydroxide to form butan-1-ol. Butan-1-ol can then be oxidised to a carboxylic acid.

  **i** State a reagent, other than oxygen, that will oxidise butan-1-ol to a carboxylic acid.

  ..........................................................................................................................................

  **ii** Name the carboxylic acid formed by this oxidation.

  ..........................................................................................................................................

  **iii** Butan-1-ol reacts with ethanoic acid to form an ester. What is the name of this ester? Give its structural formula, showing all the individual bonds.

  Name: ..............................................................................................

  Structural formula

**b** Industrially, butan-1-ol can be manufactured from but-1-ene, which is made from petroleum (crude oil). But-1-ene can be obtained from alkanes such as nonane, $C_9H_{20}$, by cracking.

  **i** Give the reaction conditions required for cracking.

  ..........................................................................................................................................

  **ii** Complete the equation for the cracking of nonane, $C_9H_{20}$, to give but-1-ene.

  $C_9H_{20} \rightarrow$ ..............................................................................

  **iii** Name the reagent that reacts with but-1-ene to form butan-1-ol.

  ..........................................................................................................................................

**c** Butan-1-ol takes part in the characteristic reactions of alcohols.

**i** Balance the equation for the complete combustion of butan-1-ol.

............. $C_4H_9OH$ +  ............. $O_2 \rightarrow$  ............. $CO_2$ +  ............. $H_2O$

**ii** Write a word equation for the preparation of the ester butyl propanoate.

.................................................................................................................................................

**d** Biobutanol is a fuel of the future, part of the biofuel revolution. It can be made by the fermentation of almost any form of biomass – grain, straw, leaves, for instance. The fermentation of biomass is brought about by bacteria and produces a mixture of products which include:

- biobutanol
- propanol
- hydrogen
- propanoic acid.

**i** Draw the structural formula of propan-1-ol and of propanoic acid. Show all the bonds.
Propan-1-ol


Propanoic acid


**ii** Why is it important to develop fuels such as biobutanol as alternatives to petroleum? What have been the negative issues surrounding the development of biofuels?

.................................................................................................................................................

.................................................................................................................................................

.................................................................................................................................................

.................................................................................................................................................

.................................................................................................................................................

.................................................................................................................................................

**iii** How could you show that butanol made from petroleum by cracking and biobutanol are, in fact, the same chemical substance?

.................................................................................................................................................

.................................................................................................................................................

.................................................................................................................................................

# 11 Petrochemicals and polymers

## Useful equations and structures

$$C_{10}H_{22} \rightarrow C_8H_{18} + C_2H_4 \qquad \text{cracking}$$

$$nC_2H_4 \rightarrow -(C_2H_4)_n-$$
$$nCH_2CHCl \rightarrow -(CH_2CHCl)_n- \qquad \Big\} \text{ addition polymerisation}$$

The following diagrams represent the structures of the condensation polymers nylon, a protein, a polyester and starch respectively. Remember you need only show how the linkage is formed in each case. Water is usually the other product of the reaction.

- nylon:
- protein
- *Terylene* (a polyester)
- starch (a polysaccharide)

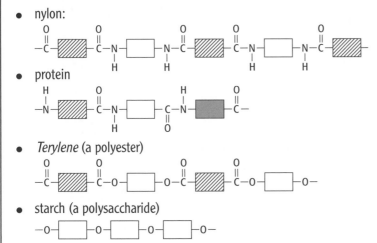

# Exercise 11.1  Essential processes of the petrochemical industry

> This exercise aids you in recalling and understanding two of the main processes of the petrochemical industry.

Petroleum (crude oil) is a raw material which is processed in an oil refinery. Two of the processes used are **fractional distillation** and **cracking**.

**a**  The diagram shows the fractional distillation of petroleum. Give the name and a major use for each fraction.

A: ................................................................

B: ................................................................

C: ................................................................

D: ................................................................

E: ................................................................

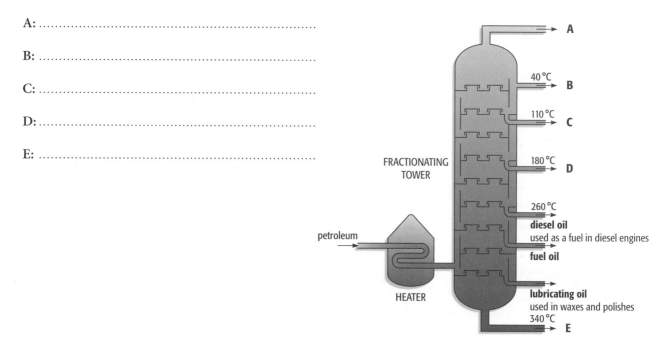

The table below shows the percentage by mass of some of these different fractions in petroleum. Also shown is the demand for each fraction expressed as a percentage.

| Fraction | Number of carbon atoms per molecule | Percentage in petroleum/% | Percentage needed by the oil refinery to supply demand/% |
|---|---|---|---|
| A | 1–4 | 4 | 11 |
| B | 5–9 | 11 | 22 |
| C | 10–14 | 12 | 20 |
| D | 14–20 | 18 | 15 |
| waxes and E | over 20 | 23 | 4 |

**b**  Which physical property is used to separate petroleum by fractional distillation?

................................................................................................................................................................

**c** Define the term **cracking**.

...........................................................................................................................................

...........................................................................................................................................

**d** Use information from the table to explain how cracking helps an oil refinery match the supply of gasoline (petrol) with the demand for gasoline.

...........................................................................................................................................

...........................................................................................................................................

...........................................................................................................................................

**e** The hydrocarbon $C_{15}H_{32}$ can be cracked to make propene and one other hydrocarbon.

**i** Write an equation for this reaction.

...........................................................................................................................................

**ii** Draw the structure of propene.

# Exercise 11.2 Addition polymerisation

> This exercise will help you practise the representation of polymers and develop your understanding of their uses and the issues involved.

**a** Poly(ethene) is a major plastic used for making a wide variety of containers. Complete these sentences about poly(ethene) using words from this list.

| | | | |
|---|---|---|---|
| acids | addition | condensation | ethane |
| polymerisation | ethene | monomers | polymer |

Poly(ethene) is a ....................................... formed by the .......................................

of ....................................... molecules. In this reaction, the starting molecules can be

described as .......................................; the process is known as ....................................... .

**b** Draw the structure of poly(ethene) showing **at least two** repeat units.

The structure below is that of an addition polymer.

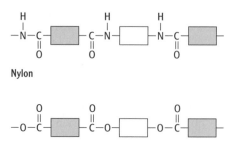

Polymer **X**

**c** Draw the structure of the monomer from which polymer **X** is formed.

**d** Polymer **X** is non-biodegradable. Describe **one** pollution problem that this causes.

..............................................................................................................................................

..............................................................................................................................................

**e** Polymer **X** can be disposed of by burning at high temperature. However, this can produce toxic waste gases such as hydrogen chloride. Hydrogen chloride can be removed from the waste gases by reaction with moist calcium carbonate powder. Name the **three** products of this reaction.

..............................................................................................................................................

## Exercise 11.3   The structure of man-made fibre molecules

> This exercise is designed to help your understanding of the formation and structure of two man-made fibres.

These diagrams show sections of the polymer chain of two man-made polymers.

**a** Draw a circle around an amide link in the diagrams. Label this **amide link**.

**b** Draw a circle around an ester link in the diagrams. Label this **ester link**.

**c** Name a type of naturally occurring polymer that has a similar link to nylon.

..............................................................................................................................................

**s** **d** The formulae of the two monomers used to make nylon are shown below.

Nylon monomers     $H_2N$—▭—$NH_2$     $HOOC$—▭—$COOH$

Deduce the formulae of the two monomers that are used to make *Terylene*.

Terylene monomers

**e** State the functional groups on the monomers used to make *Terylene*.

.................................................................................................................................................................

**f** State the type of polymerisation that occurs when *Terylene* is made.

.................................................................................................................................................................

**g** State **one** large-scale use of *Terylene*.

.................................................................................................................................................................

**h** Name a naturally occurring class of compounds that contains the ester link.

.................................................................................................................................................................

# Exercise 11.4    Condensation polymerisation

> This exercise is aimed at developing your skills in extending and applying your knowledge from familiar
> material to unfamiliar examples.

Lactic acid polymerises to form the biodegradable polymer polylactic acid (PLA). The monomer
can be readily made from corn starch.

$$CH_3—CH—COOH$$
$$|$$
$$OH$$

Lactic acid

The structure of PLA is given here, showing the link joining the repeating units circled.

Polylactic acid (PLA)

**S** **a** Suggest **two** advantages of PLA compared with a polymer made from petroleum.

.......................................................................................................................................................

.......................................................................................................................................................

**b** What type of compound contains the group that is circled?

.......................................................................................................................................................

**c** Complete the following sentences.

Lactic acid molecules can form this linking group because they contain two

different ..................................... groups that react with each other to form

the ..................................... link. Lactic acid molecules contain both

an ..................................... group and an ..................................... group.

**d** Is PLA formed by addition or condensation polymerisation? Give a reason for your choice.

.......................................................................................................................................................

.......................................................................................................................................................

When lactic acid is heated, acrylic acid is formed.

Lactic acid          Acrylic acid

**e** Complete the word equation for the action of heat on lactic acid.

lactic acid → ................................. + .................................

**f** Describe a test that would distinguish between lactic acid and acrylic acid.

Test: .......................................................................................................................

Result for lactic acid: .......................................................................................

Result for acrylic acid: .......................................................................................

# Exercise 11.5   The analysis of condensation polymers

This exercise will develop your understanding of complex condensation polymers and their representation.

Enzymes are biological catalysts. Purified enzymes are used widely both in research laboratories and in industry.

Certain enzymes called proteases can hydrolyse proteins to amino acids. The amino acids can be separated and identified by chromatography. The diagram below shows a typical chromatogram.

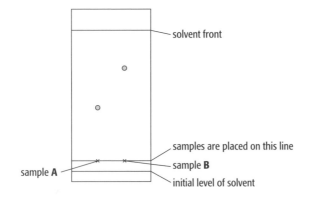

| Amino acid | $R_f$ value |
| --- | --- |
| leucine | 0.9 |
| alanine | 0.7 |
| glycine | 0.5 |
| glutamic acid | 0.4 |

$$R_f \text{ value of a sample} = \frac{\text{distance moved by sample}}{\text{distance movevd by solvent}}$$

**a**   Using the table of $R_f$ values for selected amino acids, identify the two amino acids on the chromatogram.

Sample **A** is ...................................

Sample **B** is ...................................

**b**   Explain why the chromatogram must be exposed to a locating agent before the $R_f$ values can be measured.

......................................................................................................................................................................

**c**   Measuring $R_f$ values is one way of identifying amino acids on a chromatogram. Suggest another.

......................................................................................................................................................................

**d**   Proteins can be hydrolysed chemically, without the use of enzymes. What are the conditions used for this hydrolysis?

......................................................................................................................................................................

**e** Compare the structure of a protein with that of a synthetic polyamide. The structure of a typical protein is given below.

**i** How are they similar?

...........................................................................................................................................................

**ii** How are they different?

...........................................................................................................................................................

**f** A form of nylon can be made from the following two monomers (see Activity 11.5).

Deduce the simple molecule released in the condensation reaction in this case?

...........................................................................................................................................................

Complex carbohydrates such as starch are another group of condensation polymers. Enzymes such as amylase, a carbohydrase, can hydrolyse complex carbohydrates to simple sugars which can be represented as:

**g** Draw the structure of the complex carbohydrate chain (showing **at least three** monomer units).

# Exercise 11.6  Representing condensation polymerisation reactions

> This exercise is designed to develop your confidence in understanding and drawing the schematic representations of the different condensation polymerisation reactions.

Condensation polymerisation is important in the formation of both natural and synthetic macromolecules.

**a** The monomers involved are bifunctional. They have functional groups at both ends of the molecule.

Two of the molecules shown below can be used to make a condensation polymer.

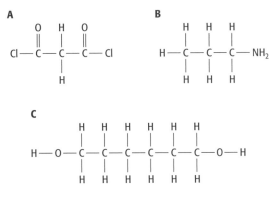

**i** Circle the two that can be used.

**ii** Explain why the third molecule above is unable to form a condensation polymer.

...................................................................................................................................................................

...................................................................................................................................................................

**b** There are various types of important condensation polymers. In each case, the reaction to form the polymer can be represented by a schematic diagram which shows only the key interactions between the functional groups and the nature of the linkage involved.

Two monomers are represented below.

HO—▨—OH        and        HO—▨—OH

**i** What type of polymer can be formed from the monomers represented here?

Choose from these alternatives:

**polyamide**        **polyester**        **polysaccharide**

...................................................................................................................................................................

**ii** Draw the structure of the polymer formed (show **at least three** monomers joined together).

**iii** What molecule is eliminated at the formation of each linkage?

.................................................................................................................

**iv** What is the general name for this type of polymer?

.................................................................................................................

**c** Two more monomers are represented below.

$$\begin{array}{c}H\\H\end{array}\!N-\boxed{\phantom{xx}}-N\!\begin{array}{c}H\\H\end{array}\qquad\text{and}\qquad\begin{array}{c}O\\HO\end{array}\!C-\boxed{\phantom{xx}}-C\!\begin{array}{c}O\\OH\end{array}$$

**i** Name the type of polymer formed using this combination of monomers.

.................................................................................................................

**ii** Draw the structure of the polymer formed. Show **at least three** monomers joined together.

**iii** Name the synthetic polymer formed in this way.

.................................................................................................................

**d** Complete the following table on the third type of important condensation polymer.

| Monomers used | $\begin{array}{c}O\\HO\end{array}C-\boxed{\phantom{x}}-C\begin{array}{c}O\\OH\end{array}$ and $OH-\boxed{\phantom{x}}-OH$ | | |
|---|---|---|---|
| Structure of the polymer formed (show just three monomers joined) | | | |
| What other product forms | name: ............................... formula: ............................... | | |
| Type of polymer formed (circle one of these possible answers) | polyamide      polyester      polysaccharide | | |
| A name for one polymer of this type | | | |
| Is the polymer synthetic or natural? | | | |

# Exercise 11.7    Small-scale molecular engineering

> This exercise discusses some of the novel molecular structures of carbon found recently and relates their properties to the bonding in giant molecular and metallic substances.

Nanotechnology recently brought a new dimension to the idea of test-tube chemistry. The world's smallest test tube has been made from a carbon nanotube. The 'nano-test tube' was used to polymerise carbon-60 epoxide ($C_{60}O$) molecules.

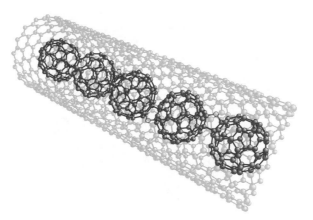

Without the restriction of the nano-test tube, branching and tangling of the polymer chains occurs. However, with the monomers lined up in the test tube, the polymer is unbranched and linear.

**a** In the above experiment the polymerisation is controlled to produce a linear macromolecule without any branching. There are, however, several natural linear condensation polymers.

**i** Give an example of an unbranched, linear natural condensation polymer.

......................................................................................................................................................

**ii** In the above example from nanotechnology, the polymer is formed from just a single monomer. Give the structural formula of a synthetic condensation polymer which is formed from two different monomers (show just three monomer molecules joined).

**iii** There are **two** types of polymerisation reaction. Give their names and explain the differences between them.

......................................................................................................................................................

......................................................................................................................................................

......................................................................................................................................................

......................................................................................................................................................

**b** Carbon nanotubes are examples of the fullerenes which are novel structural forms of carbon. Name the **two** commonest major forms of carbon.

.......................................................................................................................................................

**c** The first fullerene to be discovered was $C_{60}$, which was named buckminsterfullerene, or the 'buckyball'.

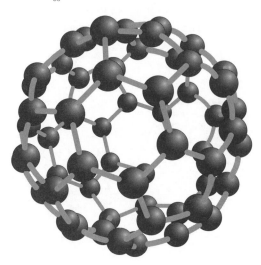

**i** What type of bonding is present in the fullerenes? Are the $C_{60}$ and $C_{70}$ spheres classified as giant molecular or simple molecular forms of carbon?

.......................................................................................................................................................

**ii** What types of geometric ring structure do the carbon atoms form into in order to be able to fold round into spheres?

.......................................................................................................................................................

**iii** Nanotubes can be built out of sheets of the latest revolutionary form of carbon known as graphene. Graphene and the fullerenes are structurally most like one of the forms of carbon that have been known for some time. Which of these previously known forms do they most resemble?

.......................................................................................................................................................

**iv** The fullerenes are exceptional conductors of heat. Why do these structures conduct heat so well? Which form of carbon do they replace as the best conductor of heat known?

.......................................................................................................................................................

.......................................................................................................................................................

.......................................................................................................................................................

.......................................................................................................................................................

**v** Fullerenes and graphene are also excellent conductors of electricity. What is the reason in terms of the bonding in these structures for their high electrical conductivity? Which form of carbon do they resemble in this property?

.............................................................................................................................................

.............................................................................................................................................

.............................................................................................................................................

.............................................................................................................................................

**d** The conductivity of these forms of carbon is unusual for a non-metal. Metals are good conductors of heat and electricity.

**i** Draw a diagram showing the bonding in a metal.

**ii** Comment on why metals are good conductors of heat and electricity.

Heat

.............................................................................................................................................

.............................................................................................................................................

.............................................................................................................................................

Electricity

.............................................................................................................................................

.............................................................................................................................................

.............................................................................................................................................

# Exercise 11.8   Meeting fuel demand

> This exercise is concerned with aspects of the use of petroleum fractions as fuels and how chemistry can be used to convert unwanted fractions into commercially useful resources.

The table below gives information on the proportions of certain fractions in a sample of petroleum from a particular oil-producing region. It also shows the commercial demand for these fractions.

| Fraction | Proportion of this fraction in petroleum/% | Percentage demand/% |
|---|---|---|
| refinery gas | 2 | 5 |
| gasoline (petrol) | 21 | 28 |
| kerosene | 13 | 8 |
| diesel oil | 17 | 25 |
| fuel oil and bitumen | 47 | 34 |

a   Plot bar charts of the two sets of figures to compare the availability and demand of these fractions.

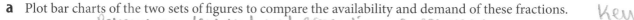

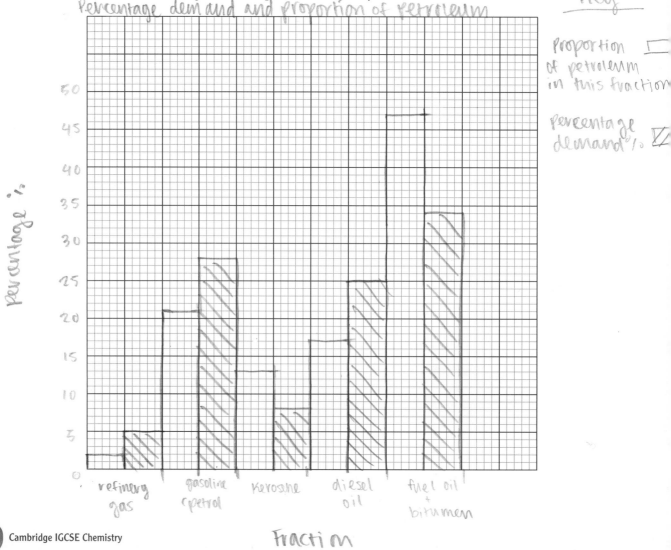

**b** The differences between these two sets of figures highlight the need for manipulation of the chemistry of the fractions.

   **i** Which fractions are in greatest demand generally?

   ....fuel oil and bitumen....

   **ii** Which of the fractions has the lowest demand and is present in the smallest quantities in the petroleum? What is the relative size of the molecules in this fraction?

   ....Refinery gas has the lowest demand, the molecules in this fraction would be small....

   **iii** What is the total proportion of the demand that is used for fuelling cars and lorries?

   ....21% is used for fuelling cars and lorries....

   **iv** What chemical process provides the answer to this imbalance between availability and demand?

   ....Fractional distillation....

**c** When the liquid alkane **decane** is cracked, a gas is formed which turns bromine water colourless.

   **i** What does this test tell you about this gas?

   ....It tells you that the gas is unsaturated....

   **ii** What type of reaction takes place in this gas test?

   ....an addition reaction takes place....

   The diagram below shows part of the apparatus for cracking decane in the lab.

   **iii** Complete the diagram to show how the gas is collected. Include a Bunsen valve in your diagram.

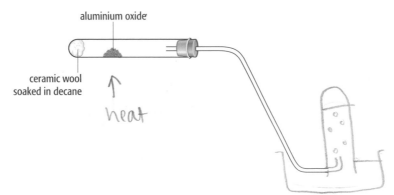

aluminium oxide

ceramic wool
soaked in decane

heat

   **iv** What is the aluminium oxide there for?

   ....It is used as a catalyst....

**v**    Mark on the diagram an arrow where the test tube should be heated.

**vi**    The moment heating is stopped, the delivery tube is removed from the gas-collecting system. Why is this done?

      ...otherwise water will get sucked up into the hot test-tube...........

**vii**    Complete this equation for the cracking of decane, and name the gas that is formed:

$$C_{10}H_{22} \rightarrow C_8H_{18} + \text{......} H_2 \text{......}$$

decane      octane     ......hydrogen......

## Ⓢ Exercise 11.9    Smooth running

> This exercise looks at the introduction of leaded petrol (gasoline), its usefulness and subsequent removal from the market. The exercise also gives you practice at calculations involving the combustion of petroleum compounds.

When petrol was first used in cars, there was occasionally a problem with the timing of the combustion of the fuel in the engine. In 1916, Thomas Midgley discovered that a lead compound would improve this problem. This marked the beginning of the use of leaded petrol.

**a**    The lead compound was made from chloroethane and an alloy of sodium and lead. Chloroethane is one of the chemicals manufactured from ethene.

   **i**    Draw the structural formula of chloroethane.

   **ii**    What compound reacts with ethene in an addition reaction to give chloroethane?

      ....................................................................................................................

   **iii**    Chloroethane can also be made by a substitution reaction. What are the reagents and reaction conditions for this reaction?

      ....................................................................................................................

      ....................................................................................................................

      ....................................................................................................................

**s** **b** The lead compound Midgley used has the formula $Pb(C_2H_5)_n$. It contains 64% by mass of lead.

Calculate the composition by mass of 100 g of $Pb(C_2H_5)_n$ by the following steps.

- Mass of lead in 100 g of the compound $\qquad = 64\,g$
- Mass of $(C_2H_5)_n$ in 100 g of the compound $\qquad = \ldots\ldots\ldots\,g$
- The number of moles of Pb in 100 g of $Pb(C_2H_5)_n$ $\quad = \ldots\ldots\ldots\ldots$ moles (Pb = 207)
- The mass of one mole of $C_2H_5$ $\qquad = \ldots\ldots\ldots\ldots\,g$ ($A_r$ values: C = 12, H = 1.)
- The number of moles of $C_2H_5$ in 100 g of the compound $= \ldots\ldots\ldots\ldots$ moles
- The mole ratio Pb : $C_2H_5$ is $\ldots\ldots\ldots\ldots\ldots\ldots$
- The value of $n$ $\qquad\qquad = \ldots\ldots\ldots\ldots\ldots$

**c** Leaded petrol has now been almost completely phased out in most countries because of the adverse effects it causes. What are the adverse effects that have resulted in leaded petrol being removed from use?

..................................................................................................................................................................

..................................................................................................................................................................

..................................................................................................................................................................

..................................................................................................................................................................

**d** Catalytic converters reduce the pollution from motor vehicles by converting polluting gases in the exhaust fumes into less harmful gases.

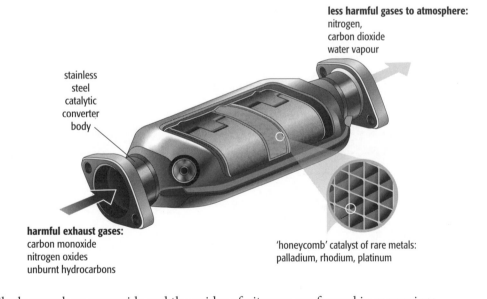

**less harmful gases to atmosphere:**
nitrogen,
carbon dioxide
water vapour

stainless
steel
catalytic
converter
body

**harmful exhaust gases:**
carbon monoxide
nitrogen oxides
unburnt hydrocarbons

'honeycomb' catalyst of rare metals:
palladium, rhodium, platinum

**i** Describe how carbon monoxide and the oxides of nitrogen are formed in car engines.

..................................................................................................................................................................

..................................................................................................................................................................

..................................................................................................................................................................

..................................................................................................................................................................

**ii** What are the reactions inside the catalytic converter that change these pollutants into the less harmful gases released into the atmosphere. Give equations for the reactions in your description.

.....................................................................................................................................................

.....................................................................................................................................................

.....................................................................................................................................................

.....................................................................................................................................................

.....................................................................................................................................................

**iii** Heptane is a constituent of petrol. Complete the balanced equation for the complete combustion of heptane:

$$C_7H_{16} \quad + \quad \text{..........} \quad O_2 \quad \rightarrow \quad \text{..........} \quad + \quad \text{..........}$$

**e** The following results were obtained for an experiment in which a hydrocarbon **X** was burnt. $20\,cm^3$ of **X** was burnt in $175\,cm^3$ of oxygen. The gas mixture was then cooled and the volume of the remaining gases was $125\,cm^3$. Carbon dioxide was removed by absorbing it in sodium hydroxide solution. This left just $25\,cm^3$ of unreacted oxygen.

**i** Calculate the following:

volume of oxygen used = .................... $cm^3$

volume of carbon dioxide formed = .................... $cm^3$

.....................................................................................................................................................

.....................................................................................................................................................

.....................................................................................................................................................

**ii** Work out the formula of hydrocarbon **X** and the balanced chemical equation for the reaction.

.....................................................................................................................................................

.....................................................................................................................................................

.....................................................................................................................................................

.....................................................................................................................................................

.....................................................................................................................................................

# 12 Chemical analysis and investigation

15/16

## Definitions to learn

- **titration**  a method of finding the amount of a substance in a solution
- **precipitation**  the sudden appearance of a solid produced in a chemical reaction
- **ionic equation**  an equation showing only those ions that participate in a reaction and the product of that reaction

## Useful equations

$AgNO_3(aq) + NaCl(aq) \rightarrow AgCl(s) + NaNO_3(aq)$    or    $Ag^+(aq) + Cl^-(aq) \rightarrow AgCl(s)$

$BaCl_2(aq) + CuSO_4(aq) \rightarrow BaSO_4(s) + CuCl_2(aq)$    or    $Ba^{2+}(aq) + SO_4^{2-}(aq) \rightarrow BaSO_4(s)$

$FeSO_4(aq) + 2NaOH(aq) \rightarrow Fe(OH)_2(s) + Na_2SO_4(aq)$    or    $Fe^{2+}(aq) + 2OH^-(aq) \rightarrow Fe(OH)_2(s)$

## Exercise 12.1   Titration analysis

This exercise will help you remember some of the basic procedures involved in practical work, including points that will be checked on as you carry out practical work safely and rigorously.

**a**  Choose words from the list below to complete the passage.

accurate    catalyst     phenolphthalein ✓    indicator ✓    measuring cylinder ✓
pipette      qualitative    neutralised ✓    quantitative ✓    three

There are situations when chemists need to know how much of a substance is present or how concentrated a

solution of a substance is. This type of experiment is part of what is known as .....*quantitative*.........

analysis. One experimental method used here is titration.

The important pieces of apparatus used in titration are a burette and a ..*measuring cylinder*.... When an

acid is titrated against an alkali, methyl orange can be used as the ........*indicator*.............. so that we know

that the acid has just ....*neutralised*.......... the alkali. A few drops of ..*phenolphthalein*.... can be used as an alternative to methyl orange. The experiment is repeated several times, often

until ............three................ results have been obtained that are in close agreement with each other.

**b** As part of an experiment to determine the value of $x$ in the formula for iron(II) sulfate crystals (FeSO$_4$.$x$H$_2$O), a student titrated a solution of these crystals with 0.0200 mol/dm$^3$ potassium manganate(VII) (solution **A**).

A 25.0 cm$^3$ sample of the iron(II) sulfate solution was measured into a conical titration flask. Solution **A** was run from a burette into the flask until an end-point was reached. Four titrations were carried out. The diagrams show parts of the burette before and after each titration.

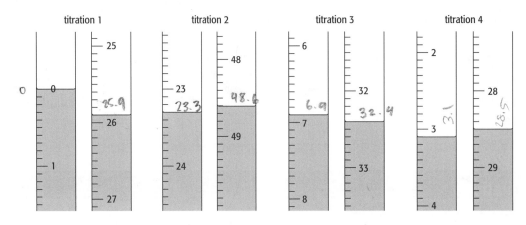

**i** Use the diagrams to complete the table of results.

| Titration number | 1 | 2 | 3 | 4 |
|---|---|---|---|---|
| Final burette reading / cm$^3$ | 25.9 | 48.6 | 32.4 | 28.5 |
| First burette reading / cm$^3$ | 0 | 23.3 | 6.9 | 3.1 |
| Volume of solution A / cm$^3$ | 25.9 | 25.3 | 25.5 | 25.4 |
| Best titration results (✓) | | | ✓ | ✓ |

Tick (✓) the columns with the best titration results.

Using these results, the average volume of **A** was ..............25.4.............. cm$^3$.

**ii** Solution **A** is 0.0200 mol/dm$^3$ potassium manganate(VII). Calculate how many moles of KMnO$_4$ were present in the titrated volume of **A** calculated in part **i**.

$$M_1 V_1 = M_2 V_2$$

$$(0.02)(25.45 \div 1000) = 0.02545 \text{ d m}^3$$

$$0.000509 \text{ M}$$

**iii** What type of reaction takes place between the iron(II) sulfate solution and solution **A**?

......*The reaction is a redox reaction*..................................................................................

**iv** Potassium manganate(VII) is purple. What was the colour change at the end-point?

Change from ......*purple*.................... to ......*colorless*..............

# Exercise 12.2   Chemical analysis

> This exercise will help familiarise you with some of the analytical tests and the strategy behind them.
> Remember that these tests can come up frequently on the written papers as well as on the practical papers.

**a** The following table shows the tests that some students did on substance **A** and the conclusions they made from their observations.

**i** Complete the table by describing these observations and suggest the test and observation which led to the conclusion in test 4.

| Test | Observation | Conclusion |
|---|---|---|
| 1  Solid A was dissolved in water and the solution divided into three parts for tests 2, 3 and 4. | ............................. .............................. | A does not contain a transition metal. |
| 2  i  To the first part, aqueous sodium hydroxide was added until a change was seen.<br><br> ii  Excess aqueous sodium hydroxide was added to the mixture from i. | ............................. <br><br> ............................. | A may contain $Zn^{2+}$ ions or $Al^{3+}$ ions. |
| 3  i  To the second part aqueous ammonia was added until a change was seen.<br><br> ii  An excess of aqueous ammonia was added to the mixture from i. | ............................. <br><br> ............................. | The presence of $Zn^{2+}$ ions is confirmed in A. |
| 4 <br><br> ............................................... <br><br> ............................................... | ............................. <br><br> ............................. | A contains $I^-$ ions. |

**ii** Give the name and formula of compound **A.**

......................................................................................................................

**b** A mixture of powdered crystals contains both ammonium ions ($NH_4^+$) and zinc ions ($Zn^{2+}$). The two salts contain the same anion (negative ion).

The table below shows the results of tests carried out by a student.

**i** Complete the table of observations made by the student.

| Test | Observations |
|---|---|
| 1  A sample of the solid mixture was dissolved in distilled water. <br> The solution was acidified with dilute HCl(aq) and a solution of $BaCl_2$ added. | A white precipitate was formed. |
| 2  A sample of the solid was placed in a test tube. NaOH(aq) was added and the mixture warmed. A piece of moist red litmus paper was held at the mouth of the tube. | The solid dissolved and pungent fumes were given off. <br> The litmus paper turned <br><br> ..............................., <br> indicating the presence of <br><br> ............................... <br> ions. |
| 3  A sample of the solid was dissolved in distilled water to give <br><br> a .............................. solution. <br> NaOH(aq) was added dropwise until in excess. | A <br><br> ......................... <br> precipitate was formed which was <br><br> .............................. <br> in excess alkali. |
| 4  A further sample of the solid was dissolved in distilled water. <br> Concentrated ammonia solution ($NH_3$(aq)) was added dropwise until in excess. | A <br><br> .............................. <br> precipitate was formed. <br> On addition of excess alkali, the precipitate was <br><br> .............................. . |

**ii** Give the names and formulae of the two salts in the mixture.

.................................................................................................................................................

**iii** Give the name and formula of the precipitate formed in tests **3** and **4**.

.................................................................................................................................................

**c** A mixture of two solids, **P** and **Q**, was analysed.

Solid **P** was the water-soluble salt chromium(III) sulfate, $Cr_2(SO_4)_3$, and solid **Q** was an insoluble salt.

The tests on the mixture and some of the observations are reported in the following table.

**i** Complete the observations in the table.

| Tests | Observations |
|---|---|
| Distilled water was added to the mixture of **P** and **Q** in a boiling tube. The boiling tube was shaken and the contents of the tube then filtered, keeping the filtrate and residue for the following tests. The filtrate was divided into five test tubes in order to carry out tests **1** to **5**. | |
| **Tests on the filtrate**<br><br>1 Appearance of the first sample of the filtrate. | |
| **2** Drops of aqueous sodium hydroxide were added to the second portion of the solution and the test tube shaken.<br><br>Excess aqueous sodium hydroxide was then added to the test tube. | |
| **3** Aqueous ammonia was added to the third portion, dropwise and then in excess. | |

| Tests | Observations |
|---|---|
| 4  Dilute nitric acid was added to the fourth portion of the solution followed by aqueous silver nitrate. | |
| 5  Dilute nitric acid was added to the fifth portion of the solution and then aqueous barium nitrate. | |
| **Tests on the residue**<br>Dilute hydrochloric acid was added to the residue.<br>The gas given off was tested.<br>Excess aqueous sodium hydroxide was added to the mixture in the test tube. | rapid effervescence observed<br>limewater turned milky<br>white precipitate, insoluble in excess |

**ii**   Name the gas given off in the tests on the residue.

..............................................................................................................................................................

**iii**  What conclusions can you draw about solid **Q** from the observations made? Explain your reasoning.

..............................................................................................................................................................

..............................................................................................................................................................

..............................................................................................................................................................

# Exercise 12.3 Planning a controlled experiment

The questions in this exercise illustrate the issues faced when designing experiments that will give you results that are clear. They will help you think through which conditions need to be controlled in a given situation so that a fair test can be carried out. They do not show all possible situations but will give an idea of the range of investigations you may encounter.

**a** **Sudso** is a washing powder which has been designed to work best at 30 °C. Mrs Jones has always done her washing at 50 °C and thinks that that temperature will work better.

Devise an experiment to discover which temperature is best for the washing powder Sudso.

...................................................................................................................................................................

...................................................................................................................................................................

...................................................................................................................................................................

...................................................................................................................................................................

...................................................................................................................................................................

...................................................................................................................................................................

...................................................................................................................................................................

...................................................................................................................................................................

**b** Harjit buys some cheap saffron from a street trader in Delhi. His wife thinks it is too brightly coloured and must be fake. She has some genuine saffron which is paler in colour.

Devise an experiment to compare the two samples of saffron to see if an artificial colour has been added to the saffron that Harjit bought.

.......................................................................................................................................................

.......................................................................................................................................................

.......................................................................................................................................................

.......................................................................................................................................................

.......................................................................................................................................................

.......................................................................................................................................................

.......................................................................................................................................................

.......................................................................................................................................................

**c** Urea, $(NH_2)_2CO$, is an organic compound which is soluble in both water and an organic solvent such as ethanol.

Urea has an important place in the history of chemistry. The discovery by Friedrich Wöhler in 1828 that urea can be produced and crystallised from inorganic starting materials showed for the first time that a substance previously known only as a by-product of life could be made in the laboratory without any biological starting materials. This finding contradicted the view, known as **vitalism** and widely held at the time, that the chemistry of life was totally different from the inorganic world.

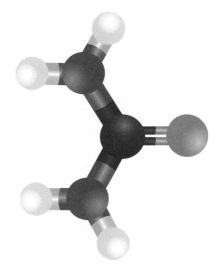

A computer model of the urea molecule

**i** Devise an experiment to find which solvent, water or ethanol, is better at dissolving urea. Comment clearly on the conditions that must be kept constant.

.......................................................................................................................................................

.......................................................................................................................................................

.......................................................................................................................................................

.......................................................................................................................................................

.......................................................................................................................................................

.......................................................................................................................................................

.......................................................................................................................................................

**ii** You have found an old bottle of powdered urea in the lab. Describe, using either solvent, how you could prepare some good crystals of urea from the powder.

.................................................................................................................................

.................................................................................................................................

.................................................................................................................................

.................................................................................................................................

**d** **Antibac** and **Cleano** are two products used for cleaning kitchen surfaces. One contains a chlorine bleach as the cleaning agent, while the other contains about 60% ethanol.

**i** Describe a test that would show which product contains the bleach.

.................................................................................................................................

**ii** Describe a way of finding out how much ethanol the other product contains.

.................................................................................................................................

.................................................................................................................................

.................................................................................................................................

.................................................................................................................................

# Exercise 12.4  Chemical testing and evaluation

> This exercise links various chemical tests with the skills of designing experiments so that they give clear answers to the questions raised about a particular sample. The exercise will familiarise you with some of the analytical tests and experimental methods. At the end of the exercise, there is a checklist on which you can assess how well you have understood the key features of this type of practical planning.

**a**  Limestone and chalk are impure forms of calcium carbonate. Calcium carbonate reacts with hydrochloric acid to form calcium chloride, carbon dioxide and water.

You are provided with lumps of limestone and chalk and hydrochloric acid together with a full range of lab apparatus. Devise an experiment to discover which of these two types of rock contains the higher percentage of calcium carbonate.

..................................................................................................................................................................

..................................................................................................................................................................

..................................................................................................................................................................

..................................................................................................................................................................

..................................................................................................................................................................

..................................................................................................................................................................

..................................................................................................................................................................

..................................................................................................................................................................

**b**  The label on a 500 ml bottle of **Harcourt Spring Water** states the following:

**Harcourt Spring Water**

Composition mg/litre
calcium 55 mg
magnesium 16 mg
potassium 2 mg
sodium 15 mg
hydrogencarbonate 240 mg
sulfate 28 mg
nitrate 6 mg
chloride 11 mg

Dry residue after evaporation
255 mg
pH 4.6

**i**  What are the formulae of the following ions?

Potassium ion: .............................................

Magnesium ion: .............................................

Nitrate ion: .............................................

Hydrogencarbonate ion: .............................................

**ii** Describe a test to confirm the presence of sodium ions in the water.

.......................................................................................................................................................

**iii** How could you confirm that the pH of the water was 4.6?

.......................................................................................................................................................

**iv** Describe how you could confirm the amount of dry residue given on the label.

.......................................................................................................................................................

.......................................................................................................................................................

.......................................................................................................................................................

.......................................................................................................................................................

.......................................................................................................................................................

**c** The metals chromium, iron and zinc all react exothermically with hydrochloric acid to form chloride salts. For example:

$$Zn + 2HCl \rightarrow ZnCl_2 + H_2$$

**i** How could you test a salt solution to show that it contained chromium ions?

.......................................................................................................................................................

.......................................................................................................................................................

.......................................................................................................................................................

**ii** Describe an experiment, using the reaction of the metals with acid, which would place the three metals (chromium, iron and zinc) in order of reactivity.

.......................................................................................................................................................

.......................................................................................................................................................

.......................................................................................................................................................

.......................................................................................................................................................

.......................................................................................................................................................

**d** You are provided with magnesium ribbon and sulfuric acid together with normal laboratory apparatus.

Describe an experiment to show the effect of concentration on the rate of a chemical reaction.

..................................................................................................................................

..................................................................................................................................

..................................................................................................................................

..................................................................................................................................

..................................................................................................................................

..................................................................................................................................

..................................................................................................................................

..................................................................................................................................

Use the checklist below to give yourself a mark for your experiment planning.
For each point, award yourself:
2 marks if you did it really well
1 mark if you made a good attempt at it, and partly succeeded
0 mark if you did not try to do it, or did not succeed.

**Self-assessment checklist for planning experiments:**

| Check point | Marks awarded | |
| --- | --- | --- |
| | **You** | **Your teacher** |
| You have stated the variable to be changed (independent variable) | | |
| You have stated the range of this variable you will use, and how you will vary it. | | |
| You have stated at least three important variables to be kept constant (and not included ones that are not important). | | |
| You have stated the variable to be measured (dependent variable), how you will measure it and when you will measure it. | | |
| You have drawn up an outline results chart where appropriate. | | |
| If a hypothesis is being tested, you have predicted what the results will be if the hypothesis is correct. | | |
| **Total (out of 12)** | | |

10–12   Excellent.
8–9     Good.
5–7     A good start, but you need to improve quite a bit.
3–4     Poor. Try this same plan again.
1–2     Very poor. Read through all the criteria again, and then try the same plan again.

# Exercise 12.5   Experimental design

This exercise emphasises the considerations that are important when planning and evaluating an experimental method.

## How is the rate of a reaction affected by temperature?

The reaction between dilute hydrochloric acid and sodium thiosulfate solution produces a fine yellow precipitate that clouds the solution. This means that the rate of this reaction can be found by measuring the time taken for a cross (×) under the reaction to become hidden.

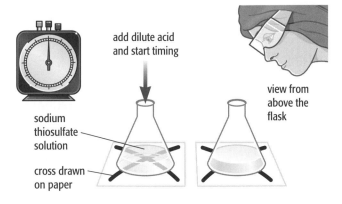

add dilute acid
and start timing

view from
above the
flask

sodium
thiosulfate
solution

cross drawn
on paper

a   You are asked to design an experiment to see how changing the temperature of the solutions mixed affects the rate of the reaction.

You are provided with the following apparatus and solutions:

- several 100 cm³ conical flasks of the same size and shape
- dilute hydrochloric acid solution (0.5 moles per dm³)
- sodium thiosulfate solution – a colourless solution (0.5 moles per dm³)
- several 50 cm³ measuring cylinders
- a piece of white card and a felt-tip marker pen
- a stopclock
- a water bath that is thermostatically controlled so that the temperature can be adjusted – flasks of solution can be placed in this to adjust to the required temperature
- two thermometers
- and any other normal lab apparatus.

Your description should include:

- a statement of the **aim** of the experiment – comment on which factors in the experiment need to be kept constant and why
- a description of the **method** for carrying out the experiment – this should be a **list of instructions** to another student
- safety – put in a comment on what **safety precautions** you need to take and why.

.................................................................................................................

.................................................................................................................

.................................................................................................................

.................................................................................................................

.................................................................................................................

.................................................................................................................

.................................................................................................................

.................................................................................................................

**b** Below are the results of tests carried out at five different temperatures. In each case, 50 cm³ of aqueous sodium thiosulfate was poured into a flask. 10 cm³ of hydrochloric acid was added to the flask. The initial and final temperatures were measured.

Use the thermometer diagrams to record all of the initial and final temperatures in the table.

**i** Complete the table of results to show the average temperatures.

| Experiment | Thermometer diagram at start | Initial temperature / °C | Thermometer diagram at end | Final temperature / °C | Average temperature / °C | Time for cross to disappear / s |
|---|---|---|---|---|---|---|
| 1 | 30 25 20 | ......... | 30 25 20 | ......... | ......... | 130 |
| 2 | 40 35 30 | ......... | 40 35 30 | ......... | ......... | 79 |
| 3 | 45 40 35 | ......... | 45 40 35 | ......... | ......... | 55 |
| 4 | 55 50 45 | ......... | 55 50 45 | ......... | ......... | 33 |
| 5 | 60 55 50 | ......... | 60 55 50 | ......... | ......... | 26 |

**ii** Plot a graph of the time taken for the cross to disappear versus the average temperature on the grid, and draw a smooth line graph.

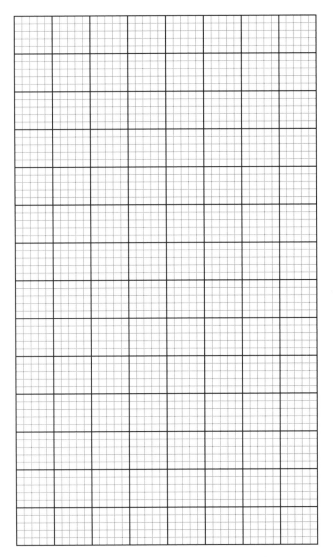

**c** In which experiment was the speed of reaction greatest? .................................

**d** Explain why the speed was greatest in this experiment.

..................................................................................................................................................................

..................................................................................................................................................................

**e** Why were the same volume of sodium thiosulfate solution and the same volume of hydrochloric acid used in each experiment? Why do the conical flasks used in each test run need to be of the same dimensions?

..................................................................................................................................................................

..................................................................................................................................................................

**f** From the graph, deduce the time for the cross to disappear if the experiment was to be repeated at 70 °C. Show clearly on the grid how you worked out your answer.

..................................................................................................................................................

**g** Sketch on the grid the curve you would expect if all the experiments were repeated using 50 cm³ of more concentrated sodium thiosulfate solution.

**h** How would it be possible to achieve a temperature of around 0 to 5 °C?

..................................................................................................................................................

**i** Explain **one** change that could be made to the experimental method to obtain more accurate results.

..................................................................................................................................................

..................................................................................................................................................

Use the checklist below to give yourself a mark for your graph.
For each point, award yourself:
2 marks if you did it really well
1 mark if you made a good attempt at it, and partly succeeded
0 marks if you did not try to do it, or did not succeed.

**Self-assessment checklist for graphs:**

| Check point | Marks awarded | |
| --- | --- | --- |
| | **You** | **Your teacher** |
| You have drawn the axes with a ruler, using most of the width and height of the grid. | | |
| You have used a good scale for the x-axis and the y-axis, going up in useful proportions. | | |
| You have labelled the axes correctly, giving the correct units for the scales on both axes. | | |
| You have plotted each point precisely and correctly. | | |
| You have used a small, neat dot or cross for each point. | | |
| You have drawn a single, clear best-fit line through the points – using a ruler for a straight line. | | |
| You have ignored any anomalous results when drawing the line. | | |
| **Total (out of 14)** | | |

12–14   Excellent.
10–11   Good.
7–9   A good start, but you need to improve quite a bit.
5–6   Poor. Try this same graph again, using a new sheet of graph paper.
1–4   Very poor. Read through all the criteria again, and then try the same graph again.